Y...
could appear
in our next
cookbook!

Share your tried & true family favorites with us instantly at

www.gooseberrypatch.com

If you'd rather jot 'em down by hand, just mail this form to...

Gooseberry Patch • Cookbooks – Call for Recipes
PO Box 812 • Columbus, OH 43216-0812

If your recipe is selected for a book, you'll receive a FREE copy!

Please share only your original recipes or those that you have made your own over the years.

Recipe Name:

Number of Servings:

Any fond memories about this recipe? Special touches you like to add
or handy shortcuts?

Ingredients (include specific measurements):

Instructions (continue on back if needed):

Special Code: **cookbookspage**

Over ➤

Extra space for recipe if needed:

Tell us about yourself...

Your complete contact information is needed so that we can send you your FREE cookbook, if your recipe is published. Phone numbers and email addresses are kept private and will only be used if we have questions about your recipe.

Name:

Address:

City: State: Zip:

Email:

Daytime Phone:

Thank you! Vickie & Jo Ann

Harvest

HOMESTYLE
MEALS

Delicious recipes featuring all your favorite fall flavors

Gooseberry Patch

An imprint of Globe Pequot
246 Goose Lane
Guilford, CT 06437

www.gooseberrypatch.com

1·800·854·6673

Copyright 2019, Gooseberry Patch 978-1-62093-322-0

Do you have a tried & true recipe...

tip, craft or memory that you'd like to see featured in a **Gooseberry Patch** cookbook? Visit our website at **www.gooseberrypatch.com** and follow the easy steps to submit your favorite family recipe. Or send them to us at:

Gooseberry Patch
PO Box 812
Columbus, OH 43216-0812

Don't forget to include the number of servings your recipe makes, plus your name, address, phone number and email address. If we select your recipe, your name will appear right along with it... and you'll receive a **FREE** copy of the book!

Contents

Dedication

If falling leaves make you smile, a nip in the air puts a spring in your step and pumpkin pie is your favorite dessert, this book is for you!

Appreciation

A hearty thanks to everyone who generously shared their best-of-the-season recipes with us.

Falling Leaves
&
Autumn Fun

Harvest
Homestyle Meals

Autumn Trips to the Apple Orchards

Katherine Wollgast
Troy, MO

When I was a child, September always meant going back to the small private school I attended. Small class sizes allowed the grade-school teachers to plan an annual trip to Eckert's Apple Orchards. As soon as we got to school on that late September day, we piled into various mothers' cars and drove up the beautiful Great River Road in Illinois to Grafton. We each got to pick a bag of apples while we sampled the sweet fruit, played and enjoyed the rolling farm hills. I loved this trip! Now that I am grown, I still try to make an annual trek back to the orchard to pick as many bags of apples as I can carry. Nothing beats picking apples on a crisp fall day and looking forward to all the wonderful treats that they will become in my kitchen. I am grateful to my teachers who started such a great tradition in the fall.

Falling Leaves &
Autumn Fun

Apple Pie-Making Day

Lori Braegelmann
Saint Cloud, MN

At our house, fall always meant our annual Apple Pie-Making Day...
truly a family affair. We would pick apples from our five trees, then
drive a pick-up truck full of them out to my mother-in-law's house. All
available family members, including grandkids, gathered there to select
our day's task...washing apples, peeling, coring and slicing, rolling out
pie crusts, sprinkling cinnamon-sugar and bagging the finished pies for
our freezers. My mother-in-law made all the homemade crusts for this
mass production. One fall, we made close to a hundred pies! After all
the work was done, we would enjoy a homemade meal together and
fresh-baked apple pie. Then each family took home our allotment of
bagged apple pies for our freezers. Mmm...baking them during the
winter was so delicious and always brought back memories of apple
pie-making day!

Autumn Memories in Arkansas

Beckie Apple
Grannis, AR

Growing up in rural Arkansas, I have many fond memories of my
childhood. My favorite time of the year was autumn. I always loved
to see the leaves turning gold and red and covering the ground with
their beautiful colors. Living in the country, there were many seasonal
chores. My grandparents had a large farm and many cattle. In late
summer, they began harvesting the corn to go into the corn barns, to
help feed the cattle in the long winter months to come. My brother and
I loved going to the cornfields and riding in the wagon as the corn was
being piled in and then put in the barns. I cherish those memories!
I remember those cool autumn nights, too, and sipping my
grandmother's hot chocolate before bedtime.

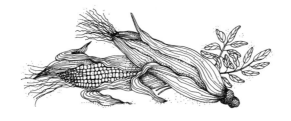

Harvest
Homestyle Meals

Autumn Leaves

Lou Ann Peterson
Frewsburg, NY

Autumn is my absolute favorite time of year! In western New York, where I grew up, the changing of the seasons and the colors of the leaves are nothing short of spectacular! One of my most vivid fall recollections, from when my brothers and I were children, is of raking the leaves with my father and playing in the leaves. We had a couple of huge maple trees at the end of our driveway which covered our yard in a blanket of colorful leaves every October. My dad would work hard to rake them all up and we would help, but mostly we played by jumping into the piles of leaves. What fun for kids! Dad would patiently rake them back up again, and let us jump into them over and over. To this day, the crisp fall air, the smell of leaves and the crunch of leaves under my feet take me back there to my childhood home and my father. My father has been gone over 20 years now, but this is one of my most beloved memories of him and my most favorite time of year.

Country Fair Time

Lisa Cunningham
Boothbay, ME

Each October, my parents, my fiancé and I drive across the state to attend a large country fair. Living in Maine, we are lucky to enjoy all four seasons and, as fall is our favorite season, we look forward to the trip each year! Crisp air, leaves crunching under our feet, a cup of warm apple cider and singers entertaining the crowds with old-time favorites are sure to get us in the mood for a day of fun. In the late afternoon, we head home and enjoy more of the spectacular foliage as we ride along. Of course, the best part is a full day spent with family. Memories in the making!

Falling Leaves & *Autumn Fun*

School Days

Delores Lakes
Mansfield, OH

Every September, I recall when I started school in the first grade, attending the same three-room school in Virginia that my grandparents attended. It was a small country school, with first and second grades in one room, third, fourth and fifth-grade girls in another and fifth-grade boys, sixth and seventh grades in the largest room, taught by the principal. Many of my cousins and neighbors attended this school, along with my brother, five years older than I was. I could hardly wait to begin first grade! The excitement of carrying my book bag filled with a new pencil box, a big box of new crayons, lined writing paper, erasers shaped like animals, a bottle of glue and a new blue and white lunchbox was almost too much to bear! My new red cardigan, black and white saddle shoes and new skirts and blouses made me feel very grown up and ready to begin learning to read and write. I immediately loved school and was disappointed to not go seven days a week! I still look back with fond memories on those days from many years ago. For me, that little three-room school had a huge impact on my life and truly gave me a wonderful start in developing deep friendships and a love of reading. I will always be grateful for those wonderful memories!

Harvest Homestyle Meals

Back to School

Donna Reeter
Vandalia, IL

I am 77 years old, yet the memory of going back to my country school in the fall is still vivid in my mind. New plaid school dresses, new leather shoes and a fresh perm! I think I remember the shoes more because after a summer of running around barefooted, shoes were not comfortable. Although the soles of my feet were tough, my heels were no match for the hard leather oxfords. I had a mile and a half walk to school and by the time I got home the anklets had worked down into my shoes and blisters were made. About that new perm, back then the smell was quite strong. One year, just a short distance from school a shower came up and dampened my hair, just enough to bring alive the scent of the curling solution. Luckily my hair dried quickly and no one commented on the smell! When I walk by a salon today, that time is as fresh as it was back in 1949, when I was eight years old.

Oh, Those School Days!

Betty Kozlowski
Newnan, GA

Growing up in New Orleans and attending Catholic school, I remember every September how Mom would line us kids up in our school uniforms according to our ages. With there being eight of us, it was quite a line-up! Even before I was of school age, she included me in the line-up, sans uniform. When the camellia bushes were in bloom, before we left for school, she'd hand each of us a camellia with the bottom of the stem wrapped in a damp paper towel covered in foil to take to our teachers. Such memories!

Falling Leaves &
Autumn Fun

Halloween Memories

Patricia Addison
Cave Junction, OR

I can still remember getting ready for Halloween each fall. It was a wonderful time at our house! Dad would be working on something in the garage to scare the trick-or-treaters with. The boys stacked cornstalks and tied them on the porch posts, strung dried corn in garlands on the rails and piled pumpkins on the porch steps. In the far corner, they put up the hay bales and set Mom's cauldron on the bales. Indoors, Mom and I put out scary decorations on the coffee table and the mantle, Halloween pictures of witches, skeletons, ghosts and such in the windows, and hung the big old witch on the front door. It was such a fun time! Then Mom proceeded to the kitchen, where she made cookies, candy and caramel apples for Halloween. I loved the smells coming from her kitchen! Best of all, she made her spiced tea for us. We loved it, and if we had colds, that tea "cured" them so we were always ready for Halloween night. Dad would bring out his invention and put it up on the porch. Once, it was a coffin with a hand that came out to give candy and treats to the trick-or-treaters brave enough to come close enough. We kids never had to buy our costumes...they were all homemade from the family rag bag or the neighborhood girls' collections of dresses, shirts and skirts for dress-up. We could be witches, ghosts, princesses, gypsies, monsters and vampires from these outfits. What a wonderful time we always had, deciding what to be and getting ready for Halloween.

Harvest
Homestyle Meals

Autumn Scavenger Hunt

Janis Parr
Ontario, Canada

Every autumn when I was growing up, once the cooler days arrived, Mom and I would go on our annual autumn scavenger hunt for nature's gift of acorns, brightly colored oak and maple leaves, pine cones of every shape and size, branches of bittersweet and soft, fresh green moss from the woods near our home. We gathered all of these special things to make crafts for Thanksgiving and Christmas. When we returned home, we always enjoyed some cookies and a big mug of hot cocoa. Then we spread out all of our treasures on the kitchen table to sort. The leaves would go in one pile, the acorns and pine cones in another and the moss would be set aside to dry. I'll always remember the treasured times that Mom and I spent together, gathering nature's bounty for our many crafting projects and then turning them into beautiful decorations and special gifts to give at Christmas. I have continued this tradition with my own daughter and am truly blessed to have such special times to treasure forever.

Falling Leaves &
Autumn Fun

Gathering Hickory Nuts

Billye Barrow
Cleveland, TX

This memory goes way back! I was 15 years old and in my last year of high school, and I lived in the country with my family. Every fall, I loaded my little brothers and sister into the little red wagon and headed for the woods behind my house. There we would gather hickory nuts, filling the wagon full. There were plenty of nuts to last all winter. We would sit out under a tree and crack them. Then we picked out the goodies for my mother to bake a hickory nut cake, which was a favorite in my household. I am now 92 years old, and every fall I still think of this special memory.

Autumn in Vermont

Shirley Howie
Foxboro, MA

I grew up on a small dairy farm in rural Vermont. We were always kept very busy with the day-to-day work that was involved. The autumn season was no exception! We had a very large field of potatoes that had to be dug up and stored in our large root cellar. I remember Mom using a big old pressure cooker on our wood stove to preserve our bountiful harvest of corn, tomatoes and carrots. Then there was wood to be cut and piled neatly in the woodshed for the cold winter months ahead. It was a lot of hard work, but I look back at those times now with nostalgia and realize what a wonderful childhood I had. I wouldn't have traded it for anything!

Family Soup Party

Andrea Barclay
Somerset, PA

Every fall, my husband's parents host their annual Soup Party. This tradition has been going on for almost 20 years. They invite the whole family: aunts, uncles, cousins, nieces, nephews and close family friends. One year we had over a hundred people! Early that morning, they prep all the vegetables with the help of family members who have come to spend the weekend on the farm. All the ingredients are put into a big cast-iron kettle over an open fire. Everyone brings side dishes and desserts....ohhh, the desserts! The soup party has become a favorite tradition for our family. There is usually a hayride, sometimes games for the kids and just a lot of fun and fellowship. Our fall wouldn't be complete without our annual soup party! While the recipe varies from year to year, it is more about the gathering than the soup. But we do love our vegetable soup! If you'd like to do this too, whatever soup you choose to make, make sure you make lots, invite lots of people and start your own soup party tradition!

Falling Leaves &
Autumn Fun

Pumpkin Festival Day

Monica Britt
Fairdale, WV

It was a perfect, Norman Rockwell painting, kind of a day. Dad had somehow orchestrated a Jenkins Family Gathering at the West Virginia Pumpkin Festival in Milton. As everyone arrived on that crisp fall day, the excitement grew. We explored each booth and shopped the handmade wares. We sampled every pumpkin food imaginable... pumpkin pie, pumpkin bread, pumpkin butter, pumpkin coffee and pumpkin ice cream, just to name a few. However, one of my favorite memories of that day was Aunt Jennifer's frequent yet random exclamations of "Wooo! wooo! pumpkins!" To this day, we still use her catchphrase with a smile when we are reminded of our family's day at the pumpkin festival.

Hayride Memories

Joyce Page
Newport, PA

When I was a teenager growing up in a rural community in Pennsylvania, my youth group from church would plan a hayride. We would meet at one of the churches and climb into wagons loaded with loose straw, cover ourselves with blankets and wait for the tractors to start pulling the wagons. We traveled on the windy roads through the country, past the homes of our families & friends, calling out "Hello!" to anyone we saw. After about an hour, we would go back to one of the members' homes and have a party in the upper part of the barn, bobbing for apples and playing all kinds of crazy games. These are all such fond memories for me.

Harvest
Homestyle Meals

High School Homecoming

Sena Horn
Payson, UT

Fall is my favorite time of year, and it always brings to mind memories of going back to school. Walking in the crisp air and kicking the crunchy leaves along the sidewalk made me happy then and even more so now that I'm older. Some of my fondest memories are from my high school days, over 40 years ago. Each October during homecoming, American Fork High School was alive with activities and competitions between the classes. Current and former students looked forward to the week of fun, all ending with the homecoming pep rally, football game and bonfire. The bonfire was a tradition going back many years and had always been the main event of homecoming week. The competition between the classes was fierce! My sophomore year, our class was determined to win the competition and we spent hours during that week scouring our little town in search of wood to make the biggest pile. The senior class had been victorious for years, but we wanted to win so badly! As the piles of wood grew in the vacant lot where the fire was going to be lit, it was clear that the senior and sophomore classes were neck-and-neck in the competition. My friends and I were certain that the seniors would win again, but then my mom had a suggestion. There was an old outhouse on our property that she had wanted removed for years. Sophomore class to the rescue! We tore it down and miraculously, that old outhouse put our wood pile over the top! My mom was happy, my classmates were happy...the senior class? Not so happy. The bonfire that year was spectacular, burned forever in my memory.

Falling Leaves & *Autumn Fun*

Drive-In Movie Memories

Lois Barnes Vinson
Greensboro, NC

I'm currently living in the south, and I often think fondly on my childhood midwestern autumn memories...apple picking, jumping into piles of leaves, hayrides. One memory in particular always stands out. Onc year, my family took a trip with close friends for an evening at the last drive-in movie theater in the state. *Flubber*, with Robin Williams, was on the bill that night. My mother made a huge tub of caramel corn, and I (maybe-not-so) patiently waited all day to dig into the tasty snack. We all piled into our friends' station wagon. We kids thought it was such a treat to pull up to a parking space, hook up the speakers and snuggle under warm blankets with that delicious caramel corn!

Dog Days of Autumn

Brandi Divine
The Colony, TX

My husband and I lived in apartments for several years after we were married. I couldn't wait to live in a house so I could decorate just the way I wanted to. Since autumn is my favorite season, I had it all planned out. I knew exactly how I wanted my front yard to look. There would be scarecrows, hay bales, pumpkins and mums, and of course our children would have leaf piles to jump in! Well, when the time came for our first autumn in our new house, we still did not have children, but we did have all the autumn decor I had dreamed of...and a dog named Tessa. We took her out in the yard and did a full photo shoot! The neighbors probably thought we were crazy when they saw us taking pictures of our dog sitting on a hay bale with scarecrows nearby, but we didn't care. We were making a memory to last for years to come!

Homestyle Meals

An Old-Fashioned Fall on the Farm

Lori Havens
Lisle, IL

When my sons were 10 and 12 years old, we were family volunteers at a living history farm in our area. We dressed in Victorian-era clothing that would have been worn on a working farm of that era and demonstrated 1890s farm life to the visiting public. Our favorite (and often busiest) time of year was autumn. From visiting with our guests to picking corn and tossing the ears into the horse-drawn wagons, we were always busy. We had spent the spring and summer months pruning and caring for the apple trees in the farm's orchard. Then in fall we harvested the apples, pressed the apples for cider, cut up some for pies and left some to ferment for apple cider vinegar. We all learned so much about the bounty that the summer of growing provides, and the tremendous amount of work and fun that happens as a community comes together to prepare for the long winter ahead!

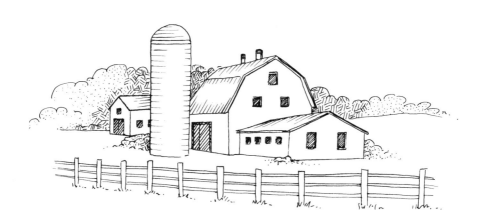

Falling Leaves &
Autumn Fun

Harvesting Memories in Canada

Norma Renaud
Ontario, Canada

We lived on a farm when I was a child. In September, it was tomato harvesting and cucumber picking time. All seven of us children were in the fields picking tomatoes and cucumbers. We would climb up on the big wagon with baskets in our arms, then Daddy would start up the tractor and take us out to the fields to fill the baskets. After all the harvesting was done, Mama would can tomatoes, peppers, homemade pickles and corn relish. Our house would smell of pickling spices! At night we could hear the jar lids popping on the Mason jars, telling Mama they were sealed. This memory has never left me to this day.

Fall in New England

Caroline Pacheco
Valrico, FL

When I was a little girl, I can remember always looking forward to the fall. My mother and father would pack all of us kids into the car and take a ride to the countryside, to the farms where there were the best apple orchards in New England. Each child would get to pick a small pumpkin, and my mother would purchase two bushels of apples. When we got home, she made the best apple pies and candy apples I've ever tasted. All of this happened every fall until we moved to Florida. To this day, I can still remember the smell of my mother's kitchen...it takes me back to those sweet memories of fall while living in New England.

Harvest Homestyle Meals

Grandma Bea's Apron

Monica Britt
Fairdale, WV

Each November, as I put on one of Grandma Bea's aprons to start Thanksgiving dinner prep, I am reminded of all those wonderful Thanksgivings we spent at her house. The excitement would build during our trip as Dad described the meal that awaited us. There would be roast turkey and baked ham, macaroni salad and potato salad, pumpkin pie and pecan pie! You could smell the delicious aromas as soon as you stepped up on the front porch of that little white house at the head of Capels Hallow. Upon arrival, you were always greeted with a hug and welcomed in. After the blessing was asked, my uncle carved the turkey. Then plates were filled and passed as the roar of chatter and laughter filled the air. Everywhere you looked, from the kitchen bar to the living room ottoman, was full of loved ones. It was the most joyous atmosphere imaginable! Then as evening fell, hugs were given again, with perhaps a tighter squeeze than before. Return plans were made for Christmas, and off we drove into the dark, bellies full and hearts warm!

Falling Leaves & *Autumn Fun*

Thanksgiving Family Memories

Deanne Corona
Hampton, GA

My favorite memory goes back to my childhood, when my great-grandparents were still living. Thanksgiving was always a great treat for us kids, we would see relatives living in other states that we didn't get to see the rest of the year. That one day out of the year would be special. The mincemeat pies that my great-grandmother baked would fill the whole house with wonderful smells. Her pumpkin pies, and of course her roast turkey, were long anticipated, but when the relatives from out of town would come, it was the just the pure joy of seeing those faces.

Red Gravy for Thanksgiving

Vicki Luna
Saint Jacob, IL

Over the years, my contribution to our family Thanksgiving meal preparation has been the cranberry salad and the pies. Many years ago, when I first started making the cranberry salad, it had a very thin consistency. I was afraid people weren't going to like it, as it had not been part of our traditional feast. As the meal progressed and people starting asking for seconds of various dishes, my Grandpa said, "I would like some more of that red gravy." We all laughed and I was thrilled. To this day, even though he has been gone from us many years now, we still call it red gravy!

Harvest
Homestyle Meals

Grandma Taught Me Thankfulness

Doug Shockley
Lincoln, NE

Thanksgiving was my grandmother's favorite holiday. It was even better than birthdays! Grandmother helped make a huge meal, and I was at her side while she worked. She told me to always be thankful for all the little things that everyone else takes for granted. I ask her what she meant and she replied, "For a complete body, for a place to live in, for everyone who fought for your freedom and some even gave their lives and left lots of others behind. Most people don't even think of those things." I still remember what she told me. I try to live being thankful and not take anything for granted.

Thanksgiving Morning

Karen Taylor
Louisville, KY

My Thanksgiving memories begin with soft pajamas in a flannel-sheeted bed, with the smell of turkey and sage dressing floating through my bedroom. I can remember as a child, my mother getting up early to put the turkey in the oven. She was quite a cook! The night before, she carefully worked the sage dressing, putting in all the special ingredients that made it so delicious. I would wander down the hall into our small dining room and turn the black-and-white television on to the Macy's Thanksgiving Day parade. Mama was bustling around the kitchen and getting everything ready for my sister and her husband to come to dinner. I couldn't wait to have a slice of the pumpkin pie and a little of the whipped cream on top. I wouldn't trade my memories for anything!

Cozy Country
Breakfasts

Harvest
Homestyle Meals

Pumpkin French Toast

Sarah Cameron
Virginia Beach, VA

*Serve with warm maple syrup and hot coffee for
a wonderful treat on a fall morning.*

5 eggs, beaten
1-1/2 c. whipping cream
15-oz. can pumpkin
1-1/2 t. pumpkin pie spice

1 loaf French bread, sliced
  1/4-inch thick
1/4 c. butter, divided

In a large bowl, combine eggs, cream, pumpkin and spice; mix well and
set aside. Heat a griddle or skillet over medium heat. Working in batches,
dip bread slices into egg mixture, allowing the bread to soak it up. Add
one to 2 teaspoons of butter to griddle per batch. Add bread slices, a few
at a time; cook until golden on both sides. Makes 6 to 8 servings.

Homemade Maple Syrup

Lisa Silver
Lamoni, IA

*As a child, I remember waking up to all the wonderful smells that only
breakfast brings. This is my sweet mother's recipe, handed down from
more frugal times. This homemade syrup is thinner than store-bought
but it's delicious!*

2 c. water
1 c. light or dark brown sugar,
  packed

1 c. sugar
1 t. maple flavoring
Optional: 1 t. butter flavoring

Combine all ingredients in a saucepan. Bring to a boil over medium-high
heat, stirring often. Continue to boil for 10 minutes, until syrup cooks
down a bit (no stirring needed while boiling). Cool; cover and keep
refrigerated. Makes about 3 cups.

Favorite Buttermilk Pancakes
Joyceann Dreibelbis
Wooster, OH

Buttermilk is the special ingredient that makes these pancakes light and fluffy for breakfast, or any time of the day.

1 c. all-purpose flour
1 c. buttermilk
1 egg, beaten
2 T. sugar
3 T. butter, melted
2 t. baking powder

1/8 t. baking soda
1/4 t. salt
1 t. vanilla extract
Garnish: butter, maple syrup,
    sliced fresh fruit

Combine all ingredients except garnish in a bowl. Beat with an electric mixer on medium speed until smooth; batter will be thick. Heat a lightly greased griddle over medium heat until hot and a drop of water sizzles on the surface. Spoon batter onto griddle, 1/4 cup per pancake. Cook for 2 to 3 minutes, until bubbles form on the surface. Turn; continue cooking for one to 2 minutes, until lightly golden. Serve pancakes warm with butter and syrup, topped with fruit. Makes 8 pancakes.

Make a scrumptious apple topping for pancakes and waffles. Sauté 3 cups of sliced apples in a tablespoon of butter until tender, about 8 minutes. Stir in 1/4 cup maple syrup and sprinkle with 1/2 teaspoon cinnamon. Serve warm.

Harvest
Homestyle Meals

Oatmeal-Chocolate Chip Pancakes
Mindy Roller
Medford, OR

My husband is a super-picky eater. He doesn't want to eat anything that is even semi-healthy! I adapted this recipe to include chocolate chips so he'd think he was eating a cookie for breakfast instead of heart-healthy oats. It's also delicious using frozen berries instead of chocolate chips.

1 c. quick-cooking oats,
    uncooked
1 c. buttermilk
1/4 c. whole-wheat flour
1 T. dark brown sugar, packed
1/2 t. baking powder

1/2 t. baking soda
1/2 t. cinnamon
1/8 t. salt
1/2 c. semi-sweet chocolate chips
2 eggs, beaten
1 T. canola oil

Combine oats and buttermilk in a small bowl; set aside for 5 minutes. In a large bowl, combine remaining ingredients except chocolate chips, eggs and oil; mix well until smooth. Stir in chocolate chips and set aside. Add eggs and oil to oat mixture; blend well. Add oat mixture to flour mixture; blend well. Spoon batter by 1/4 cupfuls onto an oiled hot skillet. Cook until bubbles form on top. Turn; cook until golden on the other side. Makes 4 servings.

Leftover pancakes are easy to store and reheat. Just freeze pancakes in plastic zipping bags. To reheat, place pancakes in a single layer on baking sheets. Bake at 350 degrees for 5 to 10 minutes and serve.

Blackberry French Toast

Valerie Gardner
Lyman, SC

My sister-in-law shared this recipe with me. It's perfect if you have overnight company and don't want to spend all morning in the kitchen. Just make it up the night before, then pull it out of the fridge in the morning to bake. Voilà! You've got a yummy breakfast without much effort at all.

1 c. blackberry jam
3/4-lb. loaf French bread, cut
    into 1-1/2 inch cubes and
    divided
8-oz. pkg. cream cheese, cubed
1 to 2 c. fresh blackberries
4 eggs, beaten

2 c. half-and-half
1 t. cinnamon
1 t. vanilla extract
1/2 c. brown sugar, packed
Garnish: maple syrup, whipped
    cream, sliced fresh fruit

Spoon jam into a small saucepan over medium heat. Cook for one to 2 minutes until melted and smooth, stirring once; remove from heat. Spread half the bread cubes in a lightly greased 13"x9" baking pan. Top with cream cheese cubes and blackberries; drizzle with melted jam. Top with remaining bread cubes. In a large bowl, whisk together eggs, half-and-half, cinnamon and vanilla; pour over bread mixture. Sprinkle with brown sugar. Cover tightly with aluminum foil; refrigerate overnight. Bake, covered, at 325 degrees for 20 minutes. Uncover and bake 15 more minutes, or until bread is golden and mixture is set. Serve with maple syrup, garnished as desired. Serves 8 to 10.

Bacon curls make a festive and tasty breakfast plate garnish.
Just fry bacon until it's browned, but not crisp. Immediately
roll up slices and fasten each with a toothpick.

Mom's Pecan Coffee Cake

Cassie Hooker
La Porte, TX

This is a recipe I got from my mom. She used to make it for us all the time. Now I make it for my kids and my grandkids, and they love it! The pecan topping is scrumptious. This cake tastes so much better on the second day, as all the flavors really come together.

1 c. margarine
2 c. sugar
3 eggs, beaten
1 c. sour cream
1 t. vanilla extract
2 c. all-purpose flour

1 t. baking powder
1/4 t. salt
1 c. pecans, finely chopped
1/4 c. brown sugar, packed
1 t. cinnamon

In a large bowl, blend together margarine and sugar. Add eggs, sour cream and vanilla; mix well. Add flour, baking powder and salt; mix well and set aside. In a separate bowl, combine remaining ingredients; mix until crumbly. Pour half of batter into a greased Bundt® pan; sprinkle with half of pecan mixture. Repeat layers. Bake at 350 degrees for one hour, or until a toothpick inserted near the center comes out clean. Cool; turn out of pan. For the best flavor, let stand overnight before serving. Makes 15 servings.

For a fruit salad that's delicious as well as colorful, combine tangerine sections, pomegranate seeds, chopped kiwi fruit, and chopped red and green apples. Drizzle with your favorite poppy seed dressing, chill and serve.

Cozy Country Breakfasts

Banana Bread Oatmeal

Elisha Wiggins
Suwanee, GA

*I created this recipe because I wanted a healthy breakfast
for my family that tasted like a treat!*

3/4 c. almond milk or whole milk
1/3 c. long-cooking oats,
   uncooked
1 ripe banana, sliced

1 T. sliced almonds or chopped
   pecans
2 t. brown sugar, packed
1/8 t. cinnamon

Heat milk in a saucepan over medium heat until bubbling. Stir in oats.
Reduce heat to low; simmer for 5 minutes, stirring occasionally. Spoon
into a cereal bowl; top with remaining ingredients. Makes one serving.

Mason's Favorite Oatmeal

Jennifer Levy
Warners, NY

*This is such a cozy, warm meal! My son loves this oatmeal all year
round, for breakfast, lunch or dinner. I keep the fixin's for this
oatmeal in pretty glass jars on my counter.*

1/3 c. quick-cooking oats,
   uncooked
6 T. milk, divided

2 t. light brown sugar, packed
1/4 t. cinnamon

Combine oats, 1/4 cup milk, brown sugar and cinnamon in a
microwave-safe cereal bowl. Microwave on high for one minute; stir.
Add remaining milk; stir and serve. Makes one serving.

Brown sugar goes so well with
all our favorite fall flavors!
Store it in an airtight container
to keep it soft.

Harvest
Homestyle Meals

Ham-It-Up Brunch Casserole

Beckie Apple
Grannis, AR

I have used this recipe for years, and it is always a hit for breakfast, brunch or lunch. It's so easy to make and travels well to family get-togethers. Yum!

1 c. seasoned croutons, crushed
8 eggs, beaten
2 c. milk
1/8 t. garlic powder
1/8 t. salt
1/4 t. pepper

Optional: red pepper flakes
   to taste
2 c. cooked ham, diced
8-oz. pkg. shredded Cheddar
   cheese

Spray a 13"x9" baking pan with non-stick vegetable spray. Spread crushed croutons evenly in pan; set aside. In a large bowl, beat together eggs, milk and seasonings. Add ham and cheese; mix well. Pour mixture over croutons in pan. Bake, uncovered, at 350 degrees for 25 to 30 minutes, until a knife tip inserted in the center comes out clean; mixture should be a little jiggly. Let stand for 5 to 10 minutes before serving. Makes 8 servings.

The prettiest pumpkins! Spread white glue over a small pumpkin and place it on sheets of newspaper. Sprinkle glitter over the glue, completely covering the pumpkin. Let dry for one hour, then shake off any excess glitter.

Country Hashbrown Pie

Cyndy DeStefano
Hermitage, PA

*This is one of our favorite breakfasts! Served with a crisp salad
on the side, it also makes a perfect lunch or an easy dinner.
Try Swiss cheese for a whole different flavor.*

20-oz. pkg. frozen shredded
   hashbrowns, thawed
1/3 c. butter, melted
1 t. beef bouillon granules
1 lb. ground sweet or hot
   pork sausage

1/3 c. onion, chopped
1 c. cottage cheese
3 eggs, beaten
8-oz. pkg. shredded sharp
   Cheddar cheese

In a large bowl, combine hashbrowns, butter and bouillon. Press
mixture into the bottom and up the sides of a greased 10" pie plate.
Bake at 350 degrees for 25 to 30 minutes, until edges of hashbrowns
are lightly golden. Meanwhile, in a skillet over medium heat, cook
sausage with onion until no longer pink; drain. In a large bowl, combine
sausage mixture, cottage cheese, eggs and cheese. Mix well; spoon into
crust. Bake at 350 degrees for 40 to 45 minutes, until a knife tip
inserted in the center comes out clean. Let stand for 5 minutes before
cutting. Serves 6 to 8.

Make breakfast waffle sandwiches for a delicious change.
Tuck scrambled eggs, a browned sausage patty and a slice
of cheese between 2 waffles...yum!

31

Harvest Homestyle Meals

Sausage & Cheese Puff Pastry Pie

Debra Clarke
Troutville, VA

When I was a cafe cook, I made some changes to a friend's recipe and this was the result. It's rich, delicious and easy to make. It became a menu item folks would drive an hour to enjoy. Serve it for breakfast alongside eggs or for brunch with a salad.

17.3-oz. pkg. frozen puff pastry,
   thawed
1 lb. ground mild pork sausage
1 lb. ground hot pork sausage
2 to 3 c. shredded Cheddar
   cheese

1/3 c. dried chives, chopped
3 eggs, divided
garlic salt and dried parsley
   to taste

Spray the bottom and sides of a 9" round springform pan with non-stick vegetable spray. Lightly press one sheet of pastry into pan, covering the bottom and working it halfway up the sides. Lay out remaining sheet of pastry; set pan on pastry and cut around it to make a circle for top of pie. Use remaining dough to complete crust inside pan; trim away any excess pastry and set aside. Brown sausage in a large skillet over medium heat. Drain well and crumble; cool slightly. In a large bowl, combine sausage, cheese, chives and 2 beaten eggs; mix well. Pour into pastry-lined pan; press mixture down firmly. Lay the top circle of pastry on top of sausage mixture. Press edges of pastry together to seal. Crimp around the edge, if desired. With a sharp knife, cut 4 slits in the top. Brush remaining beaten egg over pie; sprinkle lightly with seasonings. Bake at 350 degrees for about one hour, watching closely to avoid burning. Cool for about 15 minutes; release latch on pan, remove outer ring and serve. Makes 8 servings.

Serve hot spiced coffee with your favorite brunch dishes.
Simply add 3/4 teaspoon pumpkin pie spice to 1/2 cup ground
coffee and brew as usual.

Cozy Country Breakfasts

Cinnamon Streusel Sour Cream Coffee Cake

Vickie Tiche
Lincoln, CA

This is a delicious, moist coffee cake to serve for breakfast during the holiday months. Our family loves it!

3 c. all-purpose flour
1-1/2 t. baking powder
1-1/2 t. baking soda
1/8 t. salt
3/4 c. butter, softened

1-1/3 c. sugar
2 eggs, beaten
1 T. vanilla extract
1 c. sour cream
1/2 c. whole or 2% milk

Sift flour, baking powder, baking soda and salt into a bowl; set aside. In a large bowl, combine butter and sugar; blend well. Add eggs, one at a time, and vanilla; mix until just blended. Add flour mixture to butter mixture alternately with sour cream and milk; mix until just blended. Spread batter evenly into a greased 13"x9" baking pan. Sprinkle Streusel Topping evenly over batter. Bake at 350 degrees for about one hour, until a toothpick comes out clean. Let cool slightly; cut into squares. Serves 12.

Streusel Topping:

1-1/2 c. brown sugar, packed
1/3 c. all-purpose flour
1 T. cinnamon

1/2 t. pumpkin pie spice
1/8 t. salt
6 T. chilled butter

In a small bowl, combine brown sugar, flour, spices and salt. Using your fingers, rub in butter until crumbly.

There is not one blade of grass, there is no color in this world
that is not intended to make us rejoice.
– John Calvin

Harvest
Homestyle Meals

Mini Egg, Tomato & Spinach Breakfast Pizzas

Megan Brooks
Antioch, TN

*My teenagers are old enough to make these mini pizzas themselves.
When they have friends to stay overnight, they'll raid the fridge
to find other yummy toppings to add.*

6 eggs
2 T. shredded Parmesan cheese
4 6-inch mini flatbreads
Optional: 2 t. olive oil
1 c. cherry tomatoes, halved
1/2 c. fresh spinach, thinly sliced

salt and pepper to taste
3/4 c. shredded pizza-blend
  cheese
Optional: red pepper flakes
  to taste

Whisk together eggs and Parmesan cheese in a bowl. Pour mixture into
a large greased skillet over medium heat. Cook, stirring occasionally,
until eggs are lightly scrambled. Do not overcook. Place flatbreads on
a baking sheet; lightly brush tops with oil, if desired. Divide scrambled
eggs, tomatoes and spinach evenly among flatbreads. Season with salt
and pepper; top with shredded cheese. Bake at 450 degrees for 5 to
6 minutes, until cheese is melted. Sprinkle with red pepper flakes, if
desired. Cut into wedges; serve immediately. Serves 4.

Liven up plain orange juice with a splash of ginger ale or
sparkling white grape juice...serve in stemmed glasses for
a festive breakfast beverage.

Cozy Country Breakfasts

Crustless Mini Quiches

Phyllis Folkes
Ashford, AL

These little quiches are great for a light breakfast, lunch or supper.

2 eggs, beaten
1/2 c. half-and-half
1/2 c. mayonnaise
2 T. all-purpose flour
1-1/2 t. seasoned salt

1/8 t. pepper
8-oz. pkg. shredded Swiss cheese
1 c. bacon, crisply cooked and
   crumbled
1/4 c. onion, finely chopped

Combine all ingredients in a large bowl; mix well. Divide mixture among 12 greased muffin cups, filling cups 1/2 full. Bake at 350 degrees for 20 to 22 minutes, until lightly golden and a knife tip inserted in the center comes out clean. Makes one dozen.

Sausage Muffins

Stacy Odom
Dallas, GA

*This recipe was a favorite of my son and his high school team.
These are great to make on weekends, then we can reheat one
every morning for a filling breakfast on the go!*

1 lb. ground pork breakfast
   sausage
8-oz. pkg. finely shredded Colby
   Jack cheese

2 c. biscuit baking mix
1 egg, beaten
1 c. buttermilk

Brown sausage in a skillet over medium heat. Drain, returning 2 tablespoons of drippings to sausage in pan. Add remaining ingredients; mix well. Divide mixture evenly among 12 greased muffin cups. Bake at 350 degrees for 18 to 20 minutes, until golden. Makes one dozen.

Harvest
Homestyle Meals

Baked Oatmeal with Apple Topping

Linda Barner
Fresno, CA

*I saw this recipe featured on a local television morning show
and just had to try it! The baked oatmeal is delicious all by itself...
but with the topping, it's amazing!*

3 c. rolled oats, uncooked
1 c. brown sugar, packed
2 t. baking powder
1 t. cinnamon

1 t. salt
1 c. milk
1/2 c. butter, melted
2 eggs, beaten

Combine all ingredients in a bowl; mix well. Divide batter into 2 lightly
oiled 8"x4" loaf pans. Bake at 350 degrees for 25 to 35 minutes.
Meanwhile, prepare Apple Topping; set aside. Allow oatmeal to cool
slightly; turn out of pans onto a serving platter. Spoon topping over
oatmeal. Makes 14 servings.

Apple Topping:

2 Golden Delicious apples,
   peeled, cored and diced
2 T. butter
2 c. unsweetened apple juice
1/4 c. brandy or apple juice

3/4 c. brown sugar, packed
1/4 t. cinnamon
1/8 t. ground cloves
1/8 t. salt

In a saucepan over medium heat, sauté apples in butter until soft, about
5 minutes. Add remaining ingredients; bring to a boil. Reduce heat to
low; simmer about 30 minutes, until thickened.

Keep a tin of pumpkin pie spice on hand to jazz up pancakes,
muffins and more. A quick shake adds cinnamon,
nutmeg and allspice all at once.

Cozy Country Breakfasts

Apple & Peanut Butter Crescents

Jewel Sharpe
Raleigh, NC

So easy to make! Delicious for breakfast, or enjoy as a snack.

8-oz. tube refrigerated
    crescent rolls
1/2 c. creamy peanut butter
1 T. apricot preserves

1 baking apple, cored and
    cut into 8 slices
1 egg, beaten

Separate rolls into 8 triangles. Spread with peanut butter and preserves.
Place one apple slice on the wide end of each triangle; roll up loosely.
Place crescents on an ungreased baking sheet, apple-side up. Brush
with beaten egg. Bake at 375 degrees for 10 to 13 minutes, until
golden. Makes 8 servings.

Chocolate-Filled Crescents

Jill Gagner
Cambridge, MN

You can make these with semi-sweet, milk or even
white chocolate chips! But I find the mini chips work best.

8-oz. tube refrigerated crescent
    rolls
1/2 c. mini semi-sweet
    chocolate chips

Garnish: powdered sugar

Separate rolls into 8 triangles. Place a tablespoonful of chocolate chips
on the wide end of each triangle; roll up. Place on an ungreased baking
sheet. Bake at 350 degrees for 15 to 20 minutes, until golden. Sprinkle
with powdered sugar. Makes 8 servings.

When you rise in the morning, form a resolution
to make the day a happy one for a fellow creature.
– Sydney Smith

Harvest
Homestyle Meals

Breakfast Wrap & Go

Sherry Myerscough
Ontario, Canada

When adults and kids alike are on the run in the morning, grab a breakfast wrap and go! Wrap a napkin around each wrap and hand them out to family members as they head out the door. Everyone can enjoy a hearty breakfast on their way to work or school.

4 eggs, lightly beaten
2 c. mixed green, red, yellow
   and/or orange peppers,
   finely chopped
1 green onion, finely chopped
2 slices baked deli ham, finely
   chopped
salt and pepper to taste

1/4 t. paprika
1 t. dried parsley
1 T. butter
1 T. olive oil
2 T. shredded Cheddar cheese
2 T. shredded mozzarella cheese
6 burrito-size flour tortillas

In a bowl, whisk together eggs, vegetables, ham and seasonings; set aside. Melt butter with oil in a large skillet over medium heat. Pour egg mixture into pan. Cook, stirring occasionally, until egg mixture is scrambled and set. Sprinkle with cheeses. For each wrap, scoop a portion of egg mixture into the center of a tortilla. Fold up bottom of tortilla over egg mixture. Tightly fold over one side; roll up burrito-style. To serve, wrap a napkin or paper towel around each wrap. Makes 6 servings.

Autumn is a great time for getting outside. Place a hook by the back door and keep a favorite sweater on it. You never know when you'll want to run outside to see the colorful trees or a harvest moon.

Cozy Country Breakfasts

South-of-the-Border Egg & Potato Skillet

Vickie
Gooseberry Patch

This is a delicious hearty breakfast, served with sliced avocado. It makes a great quick dinner too.

1 T. olive oil
2 c. frozen diced hashbrowns
    with onions and peppers
4 eggs, beaten
1/4 c. milk or water
1/4 t. salt

pepper to taste
1/2 c. shredded Mexican-blend
    cheese
1/4 c. favorite salsa
1/4 c. tortilla chips, coarsely
    crushed

Heat oil in a large skillet over medium-high heat until hot. Spread hashbrowns evenly in skillet. Cover and cook, stirring occasionally, until golden, about 8 minutes. Meanwhile, whisk together eggs, milk or water, salt and pepper in a bowl. Pour eggs over potatoes in skillet; reduce heat to medium. Cook, stirring occasionally, until eggs are set. Sprinkle with cheese. Remove from heat; cover pan. Let stand until cheese is melted, 2 to 3 minutes. Top with salsa and crushed tortilla chips. Serves 4.

Breakfast foods are so warm and comforting...serve them for dinner as a special treat! Scrambled eggs and toast or pancakes and bacon are easy to stir up in minutes. Or assemble a family-favorite breakfast casserole in the morning and pop it in the oven at dinnertime.

Snickerdoodle Muffins

Hollie Moots
Marysville, OH

These muffins are packed with the yummy cinnamon-sugar flavor of snickerdoodle cookies. They are great warm from the oven, and also freeze well. They're great to have on hand for busy mornings. Just a quick warming in the microwave and my boys have a tasty home-baked breakfast in less than a minute!

2 c. all-purpose flour	3 eggs, beaten
1 t. baking powder	3/4 c. sugar
1/4 t. baking soda	1/2 c. butter, melted
1/2 t. salt	1 c. sour cream
1/2 t. cinnamon	1 t. vanilla extract

In a bowl, combine flour, baking powder, baking soda, salt and cinnamon; mix well and set aside. In a large bowl, whisk together remaining ingredients. Add flour mixture to egg mixture; blend well. Stir 1/2 cup of Cinnamon Crumble into batter. Divide batter evenly among 12 greased or paper-lined muffin. Top with remaining crumble mixture. Bake at 350 degrees for 20 minutes, or until centers are just set. Remove to a wire rack to cool. Makes one dozen.

Cinnamon Crumble:

2/3 c. sugar	1 T. cinnamon
1/3 c. all-purpose flour	1/4 c. butter, softened

Combine sugar, flour and cinnamon. Add butter; mash with a fork until crumbly.

A baker's secret! Grease muffin cups on the bottoms and just halfway up the sides...muffins will bake up nicely puffed on top.

Beckie's Cranberry Bran Muffins

Beckie Apple
Grannis, AR

After my doctor recommended a high-fiber diet, I began trying to incorporate more fiber in my recipes. These muffins are high in fiber and low in sugar...and they taste great!

2 c. bran & raisin cereal
1/2 c. very hot water
1 c. self-rising flour
1 t. baking powder
1/2 c. sugar
3 T. powdered sweetener
1 t. cinnamon

1/4 t. allspice
1/2 c. canola oil
2 eggs, beaten
1/4 c. walnuts, diced
1/4 c. dried cranberries
1/4 c. ground flax seed

Add cereal to a 2-cup glass measuring cup; add hot water. Set aside; do not stir. In a bowl, combine flour, baking powder, sugar, sweetener and spices; stir well. Add remaining ingredients; stir well. Fold in cereal mixture; batter will be thick. Spoon batter into 16 greased muffin cups, filling 3/4 full. Bake at 375 degrees for 12 to 15 minutes. Makes 16 muffins.

Call up your best girlfriends and enjoy shopping the day after Thanksgiving. Start with a scrumptious breakfast to fortify yourselves, then go! Afterwards, invite everyone back for a leisurely lunch and talk about all the fabulous bargains you found.

Almond-Chocolate Chip Scones

Becky Bosen
Syracuse, UT

A delicious basic scone recipe my family & friends love. The chocolate and almond flavors remind me of my Danish heritage. With a cup of hot tea, they're the perfect breakfast or dessert!

1-3/4 c. all-purpose flour
1/4 c. sugar
2 t. baking powder
1/8 t. salt
5 T. chilled butter, cubed

1/2 c. milk
1 t. almond extract
1/2 c. mini semi-sweet chocolate
   chips

In a large bowl, whisk together flour, sugar, baking powder and salt. Cut in butter with a fork; stir in milk, extract and chocolate chips. Mix just until dough forms; do not overmix. On a floured surface, roll dough into a 10 to 12-inch circle. Transfer dough to a lightly oiled 12" round pizza pan; score into 8 to 10 triangles with a knife. Bake at 400 degrees for 15 to 18 minutes, until golden. Cool in pan on a wire rack for about 5 minutes. Cut apart triangles; let cool until no longer warm. Drizzle with Sugar Glaze; allow to set before serving. Makes 8 to 10 scones.

Sugar Glaze:

1-1/2 c. powdered sugar
3 T. milk

1 t. almond extract

In a small bowl, whisk all ingredients to a drizzling consistency. If too thick, add a little more milk.

A quick fall craft...hot-glue large acorn caps onto round magnets for whimsical fridge magnets.

Cozy Country Breakfasts

Butterscotch Scones

Mary Bettuchy
Saint Robert, MO

My mother and I enjoy going out to breakfast together. At one restaurant, we were served butterscotch scones with the meal, and we loved them! I decided to devise my own recipe for them, so we could enjoy a warm butterscotch scone more often!

1 egg, beaten
1/3 c. whipping cream
1/4 c. buttermilk
1 t. vanilla extract
2 c. all-purpose flour
1/3 c. plus 1 T. sugar, divided

2 t. baking powder
1/4 t. salt
6 T. chilled butter, cut into
   1-inch pieces
11-oz. pkg. butterscotch baking
   chips

In a bowl, whisk together egg, cream, buttermilk and vanilla; set aside. In a large bowl, combine flour, 1/3 cup sugar, baking powder and salt. Cut in butter with a pastry cutter until it resembles coarse crumbs. Stir in butterscotch chips. Add buttermilk mixture to flour mixture; stir gently just until mixture starts to come together. Turn out onto a lightly floured work surface; knead gently until a stiff dough forms. Pat dough into a circle, about 7 inches in diameter and one inch thick. Cut circle into 8 wedges. Transfer wedges to a parchment-lined baking sheet; sprinkle tops with remaining sugar. Place on center rack in oven. Bake at 375 degrees for 20 to 30 minutes, until golden and a toothpick inserted in the center comes out with a few crumbs attached. Serve warm. Makes 8 scones.

Share homemade scones with a friend. Wrap scones in a tea towel and tuck them into a basket along with some packets of spiced tea. A sweet gift that says "I'm thinking of you!"

Confetti Egg Strata

Sue Klapper
Muskego, WI

Because this dish is assembled the night before, it makes preparing for a brunch a breeze! Add your favorite fruit salad and you're set.

1/2 loaf Italian bread, cut into
    1-inch cubes
8-oz. pkg. shredded Cheddar
    cheese
1-1/2 c. cooked ham, cut into
    1/2-inch cubes
1 c. sliced mushrooms

1 c. red or green pepper, diced
1/2 c. green onions, sliced
10 eggs
3 c. milk
1/2 t. salt
1/4 t. pepper

Lightly spray a 13"x9" baking pan with non-stick vegetable spray. Layer half each of bread, cheese, ham, mushrooms, red or green pepper and onions in pan; repeat layers and set aside. In a large bowl, lightly beat eggs with a whisk. Whisk in milk and seasonings until well blended. Slowly pour egg mixture evenly over layered ingredients. Cover with aluminum foil; refrigerate several hours or overnight. Remove foil. Bake at 350 degrees for 55 to 60 minutes, until set and top is golden. Cut into squares. Serves 12.

A quick and healthy breakfast for children! Set out toasted bread, peanut butter and fruit slices. Kids will love creating animal faces on their toast, then eating them.

Cozy Country Breakfasts

Eggs & Bacon Breakfast Casserole
Melanie Lowe
Dover, DE

Whenever I have house guests, this recipe is so much easier than frying bacon & eggs for everyone! This delicious all-in-one dish is so easygoing, you can pop it into the fridge up to a day ahead.

1 lb. bacon, coarsely chopped
2 T. butter, softened
6 thick slices French bread
1 c. shredded Co-Jack or
    Colby cheese
6 eggs, lightly beaten

1-1/2 c. whipping cream or
    whole milk
3/4 to 1 t. dry mustard
1/2 t. salt
1/4 t. pepper
Garnish: snipped fresh parsley

In a large skillet, cook bacon over medium heat until crisp. Drain bacon on paper towels; discard drippings. Meanwhile, spread butter over one side of bread slices; cut bread into one-inch cubes. Spread half of the bread cubes in a greased deep 2-quart casserole dish. Sprinkle with half of crumbled bacon. Top with remaining bread cubes and bacon. Sprinkle with cheese; dish will be full. In a bowl, whisk together eggs, cream or milk and seasonings. Gradually pour egg mixture over layers in dish. Cover and refrigerate for 2 to 24 hours. Uncover; bake at 325 degrees for 50 to 55 minutes, until center is set. Let stand for 10 minutes before serving. Cut into squares; sprinkle with parsley. Serves 6 to 8.

Serve a fuss-free make-ahead casserole for brunch...
ideal for tailgating guests. Everyone can easily help
themselves while the day's fun is beginning.

Berry Cream Cheese Danish

Tracy Thompson
Dalton, NY

This is always a huge hit when I make it. Special members of my family request it when we get together...my sister Jackie is the best!

2 8-oz. tubes refrigerated
   crescent rolls, divided
2 8-oz. pkgs. cream cheese,
   softened
1/2 c. sugar
1 egg, beaten

2 t. vanilla extract
21-oz. can cherry or blueberry
   pie filling, very well drained
1 egg yolk
1 t. water
Garnish: powdered sugar

Coat a 15"x10" jelly-roll pan with non-stick vegetable spray; set aside. Unroll one tube of dough; place in the center of pan. Pat out dough, pressing perforations together, until dough completely covers the bottom of pan. Bake at 350 degrees for 4 minutes, or until slightly dry. Remove from oven; cool slightly. Meanwhile, in a large bowl, blend cream cheese, sugar, egg and vanilla until smooth. Spread cream cheese mixture over dough, covering to the edges. Scatter pie filling evenly over cream cheese. Unroll remaining dough; separate into 8 triangles. Arrange triangles over fruit, spacing evenly (they won't cover completely). Whisk together egg yolk and water in a cup; brush over top. Bake at 350 degrees for 30 minutes, or until top is golden and cream cheese mixture is set. Cool in pan on a wire rack; dust with powdered sugar. Cut into squares. If desired, dust again with powdered sugar at serving time. Serves 16.

Planning a midday brunch? Alongside breakfast foods like baked eggs, coffee cake and cereal, offer a light, savory casserole or a zesty salad for those who may have already enjoyed breakfast.

Cozy Country Breakfasts

Best Granola Ever

Julie Dobson
Richmond Hill, GA

An all-time favorite! Whenever my best friend Amy comes to visit from Tennessee, I always have a warm, fresh batch waiting for her, and she also gets a bag for snacking on the drive home.

1/2 c. oil
1/2 c. water
1 T. vanilla extract
7 c. old-fashioned oats,
   uncooked
1 c. wheat germ

1 c. flaked coconut
1/2 c. brown sugar, packed
1 t. salt
1 c. slivered or sliced almonds
1/2 c. chopped pecans

In a small bowl, whisk together oil, water and vanilla; set aside. In a large bowl, mix together remaining ingredients. Add oil mixture; stir well. Divide between 2 lightly greased shallow 13"x9" baking pans. Bake at 275 degrees for about one hour, until coconut is lightly golden. Stir; bake 40 to 50 minutes longer. Turn off oven; allow to cool in oven. Store in the refrigerator. Serves 10 to 12.

Fruity Apple Salad

Joyceann Dreibelbis
Wooster, OH

This colorful salad is dressed in a refreshing lemon sauce.

1 red apple, cored and chopped
1 green apple, cored and chopped
8-oz. can unsweetened pineapple
   tidbits, drained
1/2 c. seedless green grapes,
   halved

1/2 c. seedless red grapes, halved
3/4 c. mandarin oranges, drained
1/2 c. fresh or frozen blueberries
1/4 c. sugar
1/4 c. lemon juice
1/4 c. water

Combine all fruit in a serving bowl; set aside. In a small bowl, combine sugar, lemon juice and water; stir until sugar is dissolved. Pour over fruit and toss gently. Cover and chill; serve with a slotted spoon. Serves 6.

Harvest
Homestyle Meals

Nannie's Pumpkin Bread & Cinnamon Cream Cheese

Mary Van Nus
Jefferson, GA

My mother started making this bread when I was little, and now my grown daughters are making it too. We know fall has arrived when one of us pulls out this recipe and bakes the first batch!

6 eggs, beaten	3/4 t. salt
4-1/2 c. sugar	15-oz. can pumpkin
1-1/2 c. oil	1 c. water
1-1/2 t. nutmeg	1 T. baking soda
1-1/2 t. cinnamon	4-1/2 c. all-purpose flour

In a large bowl, beat together eggs, sugar, oil, spices and salt. Blend in remaining ingredients in order listed. Spoon batter into 3 greased 9"x5" loaf pans, filling each loaf pan 2/3 full. Bake at 350 degrees for one hour. Divide remaining batter among 12 greased mini muffin cups; bake at 350 degrees for 20-25 minutes. Let cool 15 minutes before removing from pans. Serve with Cinnamon Cream Cheese. Makes 3 loaves and one dozen mini muffins.

Cinnamon Cream Cheese:

8-oz. pkg. cream cheese, softened	1/2 t. cinnamon
1 t. lemon juice	1 T. sugar

With an electric mixer on medium speed, beat together all ingredients until smooth. Keep refrigerated.

There is music in the meadows, in the air...autumn is here.
– William Stanley Braithwaite

Appetizers
for
Game Days &
Holidays

Harvest
Homestyle Meals

Cheeseburger Dipping Sauce
Amy Thomason Hunt
Traphill, NC

*This is a great dip for tailgating parties and anytime get-togethers.
If you prefer, you can add the meatballs directly to the sauce.*

32-oz. pkg. pasteurized process
   cheese spread, cubed
1 c. whole milk
1/2 c. catsup
1/2 c. mustard

1/4 c. dill pickle slices, finely
   chopped
1/4 c. onion, finely diced
32-oz. pkg. frozen homestyle
   meatballs

Combine all ingredients except meatballs in a 3-quart slow cooker. Cover
and cook on low setting for 2 hours, or until heated through. Stir well.
Meanwhile, prepare meatballs according to package directions. Serve
sauce with meatballs. Serves 8 to 10.

Simply a Hit Cheese Ball
Angela Mayne-Hall
Dublin, VA

*Everyone loves this! I've had to drop everything in the middle of
watching the game on TV and make another...now I make them
two at a time!*

3 8-oz. pkgs. cream cheese,
   softened
2 c. green onions, finely chopped

2 c. deli-style ham, chopped
1 T. garlic powder
snack crackers

Combine all ingredients except crackers in a bowl. Beat with an electric
mixer on low speed until well blended. Place on wax paper and roll into
a ball. Wrap with aluminum foil; refrigerate for about 2 hours. Serve
with crackers. Serves 8.

Make your game-day celebration easier
by making your dips and spreads in
advance...they're usually fine in the
fridge for up to 3 days, and the flavor
may be even better!

Appetizers for
Game Days &
Holidays

Warm & Cheesy Bacon Dip

Melody Valente
San Jose, CA

This is always a favorite at our get-togethers. Change it up
by using your favorite cheeses.

1 round loaf sourdough bread
8-oz. pkg. cream cheese,
  softened
8-oz. pkg. shredded Cheddar
  cheese

1-1/2 c. sour cream
1-1/2 t. Worcestershire sauce
3/4 lb. bacon, crisply cooked
  and crumbled
1/2 c. green onions, chopped

Cut the top off the loaf of bread; hollow out loaf and set aside. In a large bowl, blend cheeses, sour cream and Worcestershire sauce. Stir in bacon and onions. Spoon into hollowed-out loaf; wrap loaf in aluminum foil. Bake at 325 degrees for one hour. Cut the top and center of loaf into cubes or slices; serve with warm dip. Serves 10.

Use tiered cake stands for bite-size appetizers...so handy,
and they take up less space on the buffet table than
setting out several serving platters.

Harvest
Homestyle Meals

Cranberry-Walnut Cheese Ball

Amy Ott
Greenfield, IN

This sweet and savory cheese ball makes a great appetizer. Serve with a variety of crackers...your fans are sure to come back for more!

8-oz. pkg. cream cheese, softened
1 c. finely shredded Cheddar cheese
1/4 c. sour cream
1/4 c. onion, chopped

1/3 c. dried cranberries
1 t. lemon juice
1/4 t. pepper
1/8 t. chili powder
1/2 c. chopped walnuts

In a large bowl, combine all ingredients except walnuts. Beat with an electric mixer on medium speed until well combined. Transfer mixture onto a piece of plastic wrap. Wrap in plastic wrap and shape into a ball. Refrigerate for 30 minutes to one hour, until firm. Unwrap cheese ball; roll in chopped walnuts and place on a serving plate. Let stand for 15 to 20 minutes before serving. Serves 12.

Sunny Apple Cider

Trish Gallatin
Monroeville, PA

So yummy...perfect for fall!

1 gal. apple cider
6-oz. can frozen orange juice concentrate

5 4-inch sticks cinnamon
1 t. cinnamon
2 T. whole cloves

Combine all ingredients in a stockpot. Bring to a boil over medium-high heat; reduce heat to low. Simmer for 20 minutes. Strain out whole spices; serve hot. Makes about one gallon.

The beauty that shimmers in the yellow afternoons of October, who could ever clutch it?
– Ralph Waldo Emerson

Appetizers for
Game Days & Holidays

Aunt Maxine's Cheese Log

Alisa Barber
Tyler, TX

*Every year at Thanksgiving and Christmas, my Aunt Maxine
made this cheese log. After she passed away, my mom
started making it, and now I make it. It is a favorite.*

1 lb. mild Cheddar cheese, cubed
8-oz. pkg. cream cheese,
   softened
1 t. garlic powder

1 c. finely chopped pecans
chili powder to taste
assorted crackers

Combine cheeses and garlic powder in the top of a double boiler. Cook
over medium-high heat until melted; stir well to blend. Stir in pecans.
Divide mixture into thirds. Roll each portion into a log, about 8 inches
long. Sprinkle chili powder on a piece of aluminum foil. Roll log in chili
powder to coat; wrap log in foil. Refrigerate until firm. Slice and serve
with crackers. Makes 12 servings.

That first crackling fire and scent of wood smoke tells us
it's fall! Gather lots of games and puzzles for cozy nights
at home with family & friends.

Muffuletta Sandwich

Sheryl Beyer
Oro Valley, AZ

The perfect sandwich for game day! Feeds a crowd and it's so easy to tuck into the tailgating cooler.

1/4 c. red wine vinegar
2 cloves garlic, minced
1 t. dried oregano
1/3 c. olive oil
10 large green olives, chopped
1/3 c. Kalamata olives, chopped
1/4 c. roasted red pepper, chopped
salt and pepper to taste

1 round loaf sourdough bread
1/4 lb. sliced deli ham
1/4 lb. sliced deli mortadella
1/4 lb. sliced deli salami
1/4 lb. deli sliced Pepper Jack cheese
1/4 lb. Cheddar cheese, sliced
1 to 2 c. lettuce or spinach leaves

In a large bowl, whisk together vinegar, garlic and oregano; gradually blend in olive oil. Stir in olives, red pepper, salt and pepper. Set aside. Cut off top of loaf and hollow out the center. Spread half of olive mixture inside loaf. Layer with meats and cheeses; top with lettuce or spinach. Add remaining olive mixture; cover with top of loaf. Press down firmly; wrap tightly with plastic wrap. Refrigerate at least one hour. Slice into wedges. Serves 8.

Keep a warm quilt or blanket-stitched throw in the car for autumn picnics and football games...perfect for staying warm & cozy.

Appetizers for Game Days & Holidays

Warm Black Bean Salsa

Janice Woods
Northern Cambria, PA

A yummy dip we like to serve on game nights. Sure to please your guests! This serves four, so I usually make a double batch. Serve as a dip with tortilla chips or with quesadillas.

1 T. extra virgin olive oil
1/2 c. onion, diced
2 cloves garlic, minced
1 jalapeño pepper, seeded
    and diced
15-1/2 oz. can black beans,
    drained

1-1/4 c. frozen corn
1/2 c. sun-dried tomatoes in oil,
    drained and chopped
1/2 c. smoky barbecue sauce
salt and pepper to taste

Pour olive oil into a medium skillet over medium heat; swirl around pan. Add onion, garlic and jalapeño pepper; sauté for 2 to 3 minutes. Add beans, corn, tomatoes and barbecue sauce to pan; season with salt and pepper. Heat through. Transfer warm salsa to a serving dish or a small slow cooker set on low. Serves 4.

Make tonight a family game night! Get out all your favorite board games and play to your heart's content.

Harvest Homestyle Meals

Red-Hot Chicken Wings

Karen Gentry
Eubank, KY

These are great anytime, especially when watching the game. Good to the last lick!

3 lbs. chicken wings, separated
2/3 c. hot pepper sauce

1/3 c. butter, melted
1/4 c. honey

Grill or bake wings for 30 to 40 minutes, turning often. Combine remaining ingredients in a bowl; mix well. Dip wings into sauce until well coated. Serves 6 to 8.

Honey-Glazed Chicken-Bacon Bites

Katie Majeske
Denver, PA

Fast, easy and wonderful tasting! I make this recipe often, either for an appetizer or as a main dish in the summer...simply add a crisp salad. Easy to make ahead for a party. Keep warm in a slow cooker.

1 lb. boneless, skinless chicken
   breasts
20 slices bacon

3 T. honey
2 t. brown mustard
1 T. lemon juice

Cut chicken into 20 tenders. Wrap each piece in a slice of bacon; place on a rimmed baking sheet. In a small bowl, combine honey, mustard and lemon juice; brush half of mixture over chicken. Bake at 425 degrees for 13 to 15 minutes. Turn chicken over; brush with remaining honey mixture and bake an additional 13 to 15 minutes, until bacon is crisp. Serves 10.

Be sure to have some take-out containers and labels on hand to send everyone home with leftovers...if there are any!

Appetizers for *Game Days & Holidays*

Maple Hot Dog Appetizers

Barbara Kennard
Vancouver, WA

I received this recipe from a friend while living in Colorado.
It has been a hit at every party where I've served it.

10 hot dogs, cut into
   1-inch pieces
4 to 5 slices bacon, cut
   into thirds

1 c. pure maple syrup
1/2 c. currant jelly
1/2 c. brown sugar, packed

Wrap hot dog pieces in bacon pieces; secure with wooden toothpicks. Place wrapped hot dogs in a lightly greased 13"x9" baking pan. Combine remaining ingredients in a saucepan over medium heat. Bring to a boil and spoon over hot dogs. Bake, uncovered, at 350 degrees for one hour. Serves 12.

Game-Day Wings

Paula Marchesi
Auburn, PA

I love football and enjoy making all sorts of goodies for game day.
This recipe is quick, easy and delicious. You can use your own
favorite soda if you like...root beer and orange soda are good too.

3 lbs. chicken wings, separated
8-oz. can cola
9-oz. bottle catsup

18-oz. bottle favorite barbecue
   sauce

Place wings in a large skillet; set aside. Combine remaining ingredients in a bowl. Mix well; spoon over wings. Cook over medium to medium-low heat for one hour, or until wings are cooked through. Serves 6 to 8.

Hollow out a speckled turban squash and fill with a favorite
chip dip...a fun fall twist on a serving bowl.

Connie's Fresh Salsa

Sandra Smith
Lancaster, CA

When my friend and I first discovered this recipe in the 1980s, no one knew where to find cilantro! My friend Connie drove all over Burbank looking for it and finally bought a cilantro plant at the nursery. Now cilantro is everywhere, but we still laugh about our first attempt to make this salsa. Olé!

2 c. fresh or canned
   tomatoes, diced
1/2 c. onion, diced
1/4 c. fresh cilantro, finely
   chopped
2 to 3 T. jalapeño peppers,
   finely diced

1 T. oil
1 t. vinegar
1 t. lime juice
1/2 t. dried oregano
1/4 t. salt, or more to taste
tortilla chips

Combine all ingredients except chips in a large bowl; mix well. Serve immediately, or cover and chill. Serve with tortilla chips. Serves 6 to 8.

Arrange blazing red autumn leaves on a clear glass plate, then top with another glass plate to hold them in place...so pretty for serving an assortment of cheeses. Add a crock of hearty mustard and a basket of crackers for delicious snacking in a snap!

Tamale Bites

Tracee Cummins
Georgetown, TX

This hot and spicy appetizer will warm you up on chilly nights. Great for parties, kept warm in a chafing dish or slow cooker. Watch out... there's sure to be a battle over who gets the last one!

2 c. cornbread, crumbled
10-oz. can mild enchilada sauce, divided
1/2 t. salt
1-1/2 lbs. ground beef

8-oz. can tomato sauce
1-1/2 t. ground cumin
1 c. shredded Monterey Jack cheese

In a large bowl, combine crumbled cornbread, 1/2 cup enchilada sauce and salt. Add beef; mix well and shape into one-inch balls. Place in a lightly greased 13"x9" baking pan. Bake, uncovered, at 350 degrees for 18 to 20 minutes. Meanwhile, combine tomato sauce, remaining enchilada sauce and cumin in a small saucepan; heat through over low heat. Place meatballs in a serving dish; spoon sauce over meatballs and sprinkle with cheese. Cover for a few minutes, until cheese melts. Serve immediately. Makes 12 servings.

Serve warm or chilled drinks in old-fashioned Mason jars.
Setting the jars inside wire drink carriers makes it easy
to tote them from kitchen to harvest table.

Harvest
Homestyle Meals

B.J.'s Barbecue Peanuts

Adrian Handley
Livingston, TX

Several years ago, my cousin B.J. Brown from Tennessee was in the process of opening a restaurant. Before it opened, he became ill and passed away. He willed to me 4 huge trunks. When I opened them, I found that 3 were filled with thousands of family pictures. The fourth trunk was filled with recipes...I was so surprised! So, I'm sharing this recipe for B.J. I hope you enjoy it.

1 T. smoke-flavored cooking
    sauce
1 t. Worcestershire sauce
1/3 c. water

1-1/2 c. salted peanuts
1 T. butter, melted
1/4 t. garlic salt

Combine sauces and water in a saucepan; bring to a boil over medium heat. Add peanuts; remove from heat and let stand for 30 minutes. Drain. Spread peanuts in a shallow baking pan. Bake, uncovered, at 250 degrees for one hour. Toss peanuts with melted butter; drain on paper towels. Sprinkle with garlic salt. Makes 1-1/2 cups.

Curried Pecans

Becca Jones
Jackson, TN

These are great! Who doesn't enjoy pecans during the holidays? I got this recipe from a friend and co-worker several years ago.

1/2 c. margarine, melted
1 t. curry powder

1 t. salt
4 c. pecan halves

Spread margarine in a 13"x9" glass baking pan. Stir in seasonings; mix well. Add pecans; stir until well coated. Microwave for 3 minutes; stir. Microwave 3 more minutes; stir. Microwave another one to 2 minutes; stir. Drain on paper towels. Store in an airtight container. May be frozen. Makes 4 cups.

Swap recipes with tailgating neighbors...a terrific way
to try something new!

Joyce's Garlic Pretzels

Angela Wieczorek
Nottingham, MD

These little munchies are great for kids and teens as they watch movies or play videogames. Watch out...it's hard to eat just one!

16-oz. pkg. hard sourdough
    pretzels, broken into
    bite-size pieces
1-oz. pkg. buttermilk ranch
    salad dressing mix

3/4 c. oil
1/2 t. dried dill weed
1/4 t. lemon pepper
1/4 t. garlic powder

Place pretzel pieces in a 13"x9" baking pan; set aside. In a bowl, combine remaining ingredients. Mix well; pour over pretzels. Bake, uncovered, at 250 degrees for about 30 minutes, stirring occasionally. Let cool; transfer pretzels to a covered container. For best flavor, let pretzels stand in container for at least a day before serving. Serves 8.

Surprise guests with take-home gifts of snack mix or spiced nuts... in a trick-or-treat bag! It's so simple. Fill an orange paper bag with treats and gather together the top of the bag; secure with a rubber band. Hide the rubber band with green florists' tape. What fun!

Horseradish Dill Dip

Paula Marchesi
Auburn, PA

*Our family loves football! Every Sunday morning, I get busy
in the kitchen to make all the delicious goodies that
we'll enjoy. This is one of our favorites.*

2 8-oz. pkgs. cream cheese,
  softened
1 c. mayonnaise
1 c. sour cream
1/4 c. white vinegar
1/4 c. prepared horseradish
1 t. dry mustard

1/4 c. green onions, chopped
1/4 c. red onion, chopped
1/2 t. dill seed
Optional: additional chopped
  green onions
assorted sliced vegetables and/or
  crackers, chips and pretzels

In a large bowl, combine cream cheese, mayonnaise, sour cream,
vinegar, horseradish and mustard. Blend well; stir in onions and dill.
Cover and chill for 2 to 8 hours. At serving time, garnish with green
onions, if desired. Serve with sliced vegetables, crackers, chips or
pretzels. Serves 10 to 12.

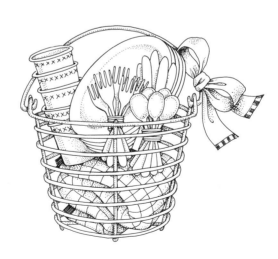

Tin pails or egg baskets are perfect for toting goodies to and from
a tailgating party. They're roomy enough to hold paper
plates, cups, napkins and a tablecloth.

Appetizers for
Game Days & Holidays

Artichoke & Parmesan Dip

Angela Davis
Guilford, IN

This recipe is so easy and oh-so good! It is awesome
for parties and get-togethers.

14-oz. can artichoke hearts,
   drained and chopped
1 c. mayonnaise
1 c. shredded Parmesan cheese

1 c. shredded mozzarella cheese
2 T. green onions, chopped
1/8 t. dried parsley
1/8 t. salt

Combine all ingredients in a bowl. Mix well; transfer to a greased
13"x9" baking pan. Bake, uncovered, at 350 degrees for 30 minutes,
or until hot and bubbly. Serves 6 to 8.

Caramel Cream Cider

Jodi Spires
Centerville, OH

We serve this cider at our annual fall soup supper that we host
every October. It's just a little different and is always a hit!

2/3 c. whipping cream
2/3 c. brown sugar, packed

1/2 gal. apple cider
2 t. vanilla extract

In a large saucepan, stir together cream and brown sugar over medium-
low heat until smooth and sugar is dissolved. Add cider and vanilla;
increase heat to medium. Cook and stir until mixture is very warm, but
not boiling. Serve immediately, or transfer to a slow cooker set on low
for several hours. Stir before serving. Serves 8 to 10.

Going tailgating? Pack a scout-style
pocketknife with can opener, corkscrew
and other utensils in your
picnic kit...so handy!

63

Harvest
Homestyle Meals

Party Meatballs Galore

Connie Bryant
Topeka, KS

My mom found this recipe in a cookbook when I was little, and it quickly became her party special. It makes enough for the whole holiday season! Meatballs may be wrapped and frozen after baking; simmer in sauce close to serving time.

3 lbs. ground beef chuck
1 lb. ground pork sausage
1/4 c. fresh parsley, chopped
1 c. cracker meal
1 c. onion, minced

4 eggs, beaten
1/4 c. Worcestershire sauce
1 T. Italian seasoning
8 t. beef bouillon granules

Combine all ingredients in a large bowl. Mix well, using your hands; form into one-inch balls. Spray several shallow baking pans or rimmed baking sheets with non-stick vegetable spray. Arrange meatballs in pans. Bake, uncovered, at 350 degrees for 15 minutes; drain. Meanwhile, make Special Sauce; add baked meatballs to sauce. Simmer over low heat until serving time, stirring as little as possible. Serve with party picks. Makes about 16 dozen.

Special Sauce:

2 32-oz. jars spaghetti sauce
    with meat
1 c. red wine or beef broth

2/3 c. sugar
6 T. grated Parmesan cheese

Combine all ingredients in a large stockpot. Cook and stir over low heat until sugar is dissolved.

Show your spirit...dress up a garden scarecrow in a hometown football jersey. Go team!

Appetizers for
Game Days &
Holidays

Texas Hot Dog Chili Sauce

Judy Henfey
Cibolo, TX

Set up a hot dog bar at your next party...this sauce will be a hit!

3 lbs. ground beef
2-oz. pkg. chili seasoning mix
2 15-oz. cans tomato sauce
6 T. chili powder, or to taste

2 T. ground cumin
1/4 c. sugar
1 t. hot pepper sauce, or to taste
garlic salt and pepper to taste

Brown beef in a large skillet over medium heat; drain. Add remaining ingredients; mix well and heat through. Serve warm. Makes 8 to 10 servings.

Hot Holiday Spicy Cider

Patti Rake
Fox Lake, WI

This hot drink is a must-have at family holiday gatherings. It tastes wonderful and fills your home with a lovely spicy aroma.

8 c. apple cider or apple juice
4 c. apple-cranberry juice
1 orange, halved

2 T. whole cloves
6 4-inch cinnamon sticks
12 whole allspice

Combine cider and juice in a large kettle over medium-high heat. Bring to a boil; reduce heat to low. On each orange half, cut slits in peel in a diamond pattern; stud with cloves. Add orange halves, cinnamon sticks and allspice to cider. May simmer over low heat for several hours; transfer to a slow cooker, if desired. Serves 20.

A notepad on the fridge is handy
for a running grocery list...
no more running to the store
at the last minute!

Mediterranean Feta-Olive Spread

Norma Burton
Kuna, ID

Such a fast and easy spread to whip up ahead of time for an appetizer.
It disappears fast! I've been known to double the recipe when our
adult kids come to visit.

6-oz. container crumbled
    feta cheese
1 c. sour cream
4 cloves garlic, chopped
15-1/2 oz. can garbanzo beans,
    drained and rinsed
1 T. lemon juice
1/2 c. olive oil

1/2 to 3/4 c. Kalamata olives,
    pitted and coarsely chopped
1/2 bunch fresh parsley, coarsely
    chopped
pepper to taste
pita chips, baguette slices and/or
    cut-up fresh vegetables

Crumble cheese into a food processor; add sour cream, garlic and beans.
Process until smooth; pulse in lemon juice and olive oil. Fold in olives
and parsley; season with pepper. Spread mixture into a serving dish.
Cover and chill for 2 hours to allow flavors to mingle. Serve with pita
chips, baguette slices and vegetables. Serves 8 to 10.

Tag sales and flea markets are the best places to find tea cups,
mugs and even kid-size cups. Mixing and matching colors and
patterns for serving tea, cocoa or punch is half the fun!

Appetizers for
Game Days &
Holidays

Roasted Red Pepper & Artichoke Dip

Lori Rosenberg
University Heights, OH

When I found a similar recipe, I added some of my own touches. It has become an instant favorite for game-day get-togethers, both large and small!

8-oz. pkg. cream cheese, softened
8-oz. container sour cream
1 c. shredded mozzarella cheese
1/2 c. grated Parmesan cheese
13-oz. jar marinated artichoke hearts, drained and quartered

12-oz. jar roasted red peppers, drained and chopped
1/2 c. banana peppers, chopped
5 cloves garlic, chopped
toasted baguette slices

Melt cream cheese in a large skillet over low heat, stirring until smooth. Remove from heat. Stir in sour cream, mozzarella cheese and Parmesan cheese, blending well. Return to medium-low heat. Stir in remaining ingredients except baguettes; heat through. Serve warm with toasted baguette slices. Serves 12.

Try serving "light" dippers with hearty full-flavored dips and spreads. Bite-size baby vegetables, pita wedges, baked tortilla chips and multi-grain crispbread are all sturdy enough to scoop, yet won't overshadow the flavor of the dip.

Cranberry-Orange Snack Mix

Susan Kruspe
Hall, NY

This has a sweeter taste than traditional party mix, and the cranberries give it a festive color! Feel free to mix & match the cereals, as long as you have nine cups total. I have also added doughnut-shaped oat cereal and cheese crackers.

3 c. bite-size crispy corn cereal squares
3 c. bite-size crispy rice cereal squares
3 c. bite-size crispy wheat cereal squares
1 c. sliced almonds or other nuts

1 c. pretzel rings or sticks
1/4 c. butter, sliced
1/4 c. brown sugar, packed
1/4 c. frozen orange juice concentrate, thawed
1 c. dried cranberries
1 c. white chocolate chips

In a large bowl, mix cereals, nuts and pretzels; set aside. In a microwave-safe bowl, combine butter, brown sugar and orange juice. Microwave on high for 20 seconds; stir. Pour over cereal mixture; stir until evenly coated. Pour cereal mixture into a lightly greased large roasting pan. Bake, uncovered, at 300 degrees for 30 minutes, stirring after 15 minutes. Remove from oven; cool completely. Stir in cranberries and chocolate chips. Store in an airtight container. Makes 11 cups.

Back-to-school time isn't just for kids. Treat yourself to a class that you've been longing to try...whether it's knitting, cooking, yoga or even a foreign language. Take along a friend for twice the fun!

Appetizers for
Game Days & Holidays

Jojo's Fruit Party Punch

JoAnn Vladimiroff
Cartersville, GA

*I made this punch for a holiday party and it was such a hit,
everyone wanted the recipe! The fruit-filled ice ring is
easy to make and looks so nice in the punch bowl.*

2 11-1/2 oz. cans frozen
  orange pineapple-apple juice
  concentrate, divided
6 c. water, divided
11-oz. can mandarin oranges,
  drained
8-oz. can crushed pineapple,
  drained

1 c. fresh or frozen strawberries,
  hulled and quartered
2-ltr. bottle pineapple soda,
  chilled
2-ltr. bottle grapefruit soda,
  chilled
1/2 pt. rainbow sherbet

A day or two ahead of time, combine one can juice concentrate,
2-1/2 cups water and all fruit in a large pitcher; stir well. Pour into a
gelatin mold or ring; freeze. Shortly before serving time, combine
remaining can of juice and remaining water in a large punch bowl.
Add sodas; carefully add frozen fruit ring and scoops of sherbet. Makes
40 servings.

Stir up some Grizzly Gorp for munching on hikes and tucking
into lunchboxes. Just toss together 2 cups bear-shaped graham
crackers, one cup mini marshmallows, one cup peanuts and
1/2 cup golden raisins. Yum!

Quebec Maple Dip

Mitzy LaFrenais-Hafner
Quebec, Canada

A Quebec favorite! This dip is great with sliced fresh vegetables, and can also be served with chicken, fish, shellfish or fresh-cut fried potato wedges. So versatile and good!

1 c. mayonnaise
1/2 c. plain Greek yogurt
1/4 c. pure maple syrup
2 T. Dijon mustard
2 T. fresh parsley, chopped

3 T. fresh chives, chopped
2 T. fresh basil, chopped
3 cloves garlic, minced
salt and pepper to taste

Combine mayonnaise and yogurt in a bowl; mix well. Stir in remaining ingredients, seasoning generously with salt and pepper. Cover and let stand at least 30 minutes before serving to allow the flavors to blend. Serves 4 to 6.

Pack dips and sauces in little lidded Mason jars to take along to autumn picnics. Veggie and snack sticks are easy to dip right into the jars. Try pretzel sticks or apple slices with caramel dip and marshmallows with chocolate dip...yum!

Appetizers for *Game Days & Holidays*

Apple Cider-Bacon Cheese Ball

Andrea Heyart
Savannah, TX

This cheese ball is as delicious as it is unusual! The apple cider lends just the right flavor for a salty-sweet combination.

8-oz. pkg. cream cheese,
  softened
1/4 c. mayonnaise
1/2 c. apple cider, divided
2 T. fresh chives, minced

16-oz. pkg. shredded sharp
  Cheddar cheese
5 to 6 slices bacon, crisply
  cooked and crumbled
snack crackers

In a bowl, with an electric mixer on medium speed, beat together cream cheese, mayonnaise and cider until smooth and fluffy. Add remaining ingredients except crackers, beating until well combined. Shape into one or 2 balls; cover tightly with plastic wrap. Refrigerate overnight, or until firm. Serve with crackers. Makes 15 servings.

Pumpkin Pie Cheesecake Spread

Jenita Davison
La Plata, MO

This spread is really good on vanilla wafers or graham crackers. All the spice of pumpkin pie, but so easy to mix, serve and eat! The spices can be adjusted to individual taste. Use dark brown sugar for a more intense flavor.

8-oz. pkg. cream cheese,
  softened
2 T. light brown sugar, packed
1/4 t. maple extract
1/4 t. cinnamon

1/4 t. nutmeg
1/8 t. ground ginger
1/8 t. ground cloves
graham crackers or vanilla
  wafers

In a bowl, with an electric mixer on medium speed, beat cream cheese until fluffy. Beat in brown sugar, extract and spices; transfer to a serving bowl. Cover and let stand for one hour before serving to allow flavors to combine. Serve with graham crackers or vanilla wafers. Makes 12 servings.

Harvest
Homestyle Meals

Oriental Glazed Riblets

Margaret Welder
Madrid, IA

My husband loves these! This recipe came from an adult education class I took in the 1970s. I often serve them as a main dish instead of as an appetizer. They are delicious and unique at the same time.

1-1/2 lbs. pork riblets, rinsed
  and cut apart
1/4 c. soy sauce, divided
3 T. dry sherry or water, divided
2 T. plus 1 t. sugar, divided

1/2 t. 5-spice powder
1-1/2 c. boiling water
1 clove garlic, minced
3 T. peanut oil

In a large container, combine riblets, 2 tablespoons soy sauce, one tablespoon sherry or water, one teaspoon sugar and 5-spice powder. Stir well; let stand for 15 minutes. Transfer riblets and soy sauce mixture into a large saucepan; add boiling water. Bring to a boil over medium-high heat. Reduce heat to low; simmer for 15 minutes, or until riblets are tender but not falling off the bone. Drain, reserving 1/4 cup of liquid in pan. Add remaining soy sauce and sherry or water to reserved liquid in pan; set aside. In a wok or deep skillet, heat oil and garlic over medium heat. Add remaining sugar; stir until dissolved. Slowly and carefully stir in reserved liquid; add riblets. Continue to cook and stir until no liquid remains. Serve hot. Serves 3 to 4.

"Sandwich sushi" is sure to be a hit for after-school snacking or in lunchboxes. Spread tortillas with cream cheese and layer on sliced deli meat and spinach leaves, or other favorite foods...there are lots of possibilities. Roll up tightly and slice into easy-to-handle pieces.

Appetizers for *Game Days & Holidays*

Buffalo Chicken Pinwheels

JoAnn
Gooseberry Patch

Tortilla pinwheels are a favorite of ours for parties. So easy to make...so good to eat! I like to use different colors of tortillas for a little variety.

2 8-oz. pkgs. cream cheese,
   softened
1-oz. pkg. ranch salad
   dressing mix
1/2 c. buffalo wing sauce
1 c. shredded Cheddar cheese
1 c. green onions, chopped

1-1/2 c. cooked chicken,
   shredded, or 2 5-oz. cans
   chicken, drained and flaked
6 10-inch flour tortillas
Garnish: ranch or blue cheese
   salad dressing

Combine cream cheese and salad dressing mix in a large bowl. Beat with an electric mixer on medium speed until well blended; beat in wing sauce. Stir in cheese, onions and chicken. Spread mixture evenly over tortillas. Roll up tightly; cover with plastic and chill for 3 hours. Cut into one-inch slices, fasten with toothpicks, if desired. Serve with salad dressing for dipping. Makes about 5 dozen.

Reduced-fat cream cheese is an easy substitute for the full-fat version in appetizer recipes. Flavor and texture may vary from brand to brand...you're sure to find one that you like just as much as the "real thing."

Antipasto Cheese Ball

Vicki Lund
Huntington, WV

My son's Cub Scout den was having a Halloween party, and we were asked to bring cheese and crackers. I started thinking about something fun and delicious for the kids as well as the adults, and that's how Antipasto Cheese Ball was born. I took it to the gathering and within ten minutes it was all gone...I overheard people saying, "That cheese ball was out of this world!"

2 8-oz. pkg. cream cheese, softened
1-oz. pkg ranch salad dressing mix
1 T. Italian seasoning
1/8 to 1/4 t. seasoned salt
pepper to taste
Optional: red pepper flakes to taste
1/2 c. mayonnaise
1 c. carrots, peeled and finely chopped
3 green onions, sliced on the diagonal
1 c. cauliflower, finely chopped
15 green olives, finely chopped
1-1/4 c. mixed green, red and yellow peppers, finely chopped
1/4 c. pepperoncini peppers, finely chopped
6 slices bacon, crisply cooked and crumbled
2 3-1/2 oz. pkgs. pepperoni, finely chopped and divided
shredded wheat crackers or thin wheat crackers

Place cream cheese in a large bowl; sprinkle with salad dressing mix and seasonings. Mix until well blended. Add mayonnaise, vegetables, bacon and half of pepperoni; mix will. Cover and chill for one hour, or until firm; shape into a ball. Roll in remaining pepperoni to coat. Wrap in plastic wrap; refrigerate. At serving time, let stand at room temperature for about 20 minutes. Serve with crackers. Serves 20.

Appetizers for Game Days & Holidays

Shrimp & Crab Layered Dip

Cathy Newbrough
Lebanon, MO

Delicious, but so simple to make! Great for office carry-in parties.

8-oz. pkg. cream cheese,
   softened
12-oz. bottle chili sauce
4-1/4 oz. can small shrimp,
   drained
4-1/4 oz. can crabmeat, drained
   and flaked

1 c. green pepper, chopped
5 to 6 green onions, chopped
3-oz. can sliced black olives,
   drained
1 to 2 8-oz. pkgs. shredded
   Cheddar cheese
snack crackers

Spread cream cheese on a snack plate; spread chili sauce over cream cheese. Sprinkle with shrimp, crabmeat and vegetables; top with shredded cheese. Cover and chill until serving time. Serve with crackers. Serves 12.

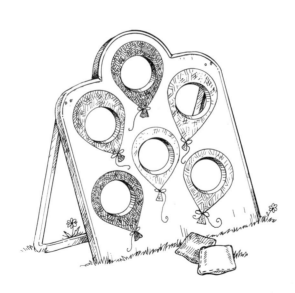

Host a neighborhood block party. Invite everyone to bring their own specialty to share, like chili, chicken wings or barbecued ribs. You provide the beverages, baskets of warm cornbread and plenty of napkins. Sure to be fun for all!

Harvest
Homestyle Meals

Tasty Taco Tarts

Karen Wilson
Defiance, OH

All the Mexican flavors we love, in easy-to-eat morsels.

1 lb. ground beef chuck
2 T. taco seasoning mix
2 T. ice water
1 c. shredded Cheddar cheese
1 c. sour cream
2 T. taco sauce

2 T. chopped black olives,
    drained
3/4 c. tortilla chips, coarsely
    chopped
Optional: salsa, sour cream

Mix beef, taco seasoning, ice water and cheese. Press mixture into the
bottom and sides of 36 greased mini tart shell pans. In a separate bowl,
combine sour cream, taco sauce, olives and crushed tortilla chips.
Spoon into shells, mounding slightly. Bake at 425 degrees for 8 to
10 minutes. Serve hot, garnished with salsa and sour cream, if desired.
Makes 3 dozen.

Hot & Bubbly Cheese Dip

Lee Smith
Pembroke Pines, FL

Once you start eating it, it's impossible to stop...enjoy!

1 large round loaf bread
2 8-oz. pkgs. cream cheese,
    softened
8-oz. pkg. shredded Parmesan
    cheese

8-oz. pkg. shredded mozzarella
    cheese
16-oz. jar mayonnaise
Optional: crackers, tortilla chips

Hollow out loaf; cut pulled-out bread into small cubes and set aside. In a
bowl, combine cheeses and mayonnaise. Spoon mixture into loaf; set on
a baking sheet. Bake at 350 degrees for 30 to 40 minutes, until bubbly
and golden. Place loaf on a serving plate; surround with bread cubes.
May also serve with crackers or chips. Serves 12.

Appetizers for *Game Days & Holidays*

Sweet-and-Sour Mini Hot Dogs

Joy Williams
Woodlynne, NJ

*My mom used this recipe when she hosted parties for friends.
It is so good! Before every party was over, the hot dogs
were all gone and everyone wanted the recipe.*

12-oz. jar apple jelly
1 T. Dijon mustard
1 T. cider vinegar

14-oz. pkg. mini cocktail
  hot dogs

In a large saucepan over low heat, combine jelly, mustard and vinegar.
Cook and stir until jelly is melted; keep stirring to a rolling boil. Add hot
dogs; cook on low heat until jelly mixture thickens and hot dogs darken.
Transfer to a serving bowl; serve warm. Serves 8 to 12.

Pita Party Pizzas

Mel Chencharick
Julian, PA

*With football season here, I love to find great snacks to make
while we watch the game. Anything pizza is sure to be a winner!
These are easy, quick and really good.*

2 7-oz. pkgs. mini pitas, split
14-oz. jar pizza sauce
2 8-oz. pkgs. shredded
  mozzarella cheese

10 slices bacon, crisply cooked
  and crumbled
3-1/2 oz. pkg. sliced pepperoni,
  chopped, or mini pepperoni

Arrange pita halves on 2 parchment paper-lined baking sheets. Spread
pizza sauce evenly over pitas. Sprinkle with cheese; top with bacon and
pepperoni. Bake at 400 degrees for 10 to 12 minutes, until cheese is
melted. Makes 4 dozen.

Spicy-Hot Party Mix

Diana Krol
Hutchinson, KS

My youngest son would much rather have this party mix than any dessert or cookie! When he was in college, I'd send him a batch to get him through finals week. I always make it for the holidays and often gift containers filled with it at Christmas. Enjoy it by the handful! It's a family favorite...I bet you'll like it too!

14-oz. pkg. bite-size crispy
   corn cereal squares
12.8-oz. pkg. bite-size crispy
   rice cereal squares
7-oz. doughnut-shaped
   oat cereal
16-oz. jar dry-roasted peanuts
16-oz. pkg. mini pretzels

1 c. butter, melted
1/2 c. Worcestershire sauce
2 T. seasoned salt
2 T. Creole seasoning
1 T. garlic powder
1 T. onion powder
1 T. chili powder
1 T. cayenne powder

In a large roasting pan, combine cereal, nuts and pretzels; gently stir together. In a bowl, combine melted butter, Worcestershire sauce and spices; mix well. Pour over cereal mixture; gently fold in. Bake at 300 degrees for 1-1/2 hours, stirring every 15 minutes. Remove from oven; let cool. Store in a tightly covered container. Makes 20 servings.

White paper coffee filters make tidy toss-away holders for party mix and popcorn as well as sandwiches and tacos.

Appetizers for
Game Days &
Holidays

Kent's Fire Crackers

Laura Kent
Houston, TX

Our Pits & Ashes cook-off team makes about 20 boxes of these tasty crackers to serve at the Houston Livestock Show & Rodeo BBQ cook-off! Spicy and yummy...everyone loves them.

16-oz. pkg. saltine crackers
2 c. canola oil
2 T. red pepper flakes

2-oz. pkg. ranch salad dressing
   mix

Transfer crackers to a 2-gallon plastic zipping bag. Place inside a second bag (to prevent oil leakage) and set aside. Whisk together together oil, red pepper flakes and salad dressing mix; pour over crackers. Press air out of inner bag and seal. Carefully turn bag until all crackers are coated. For best flavor, turn bag again, 4 to 5 times a day, for 5 to 7 days before serving. Serves 20.

Autumn Spice Pumpkin Seeds

Carol Baize
Canton, OH

When cleaning out that special Jack-o'-Lantern, save those precious seeds! They make a great fall snack.

1-1/2 T. butter, melted
1/2 t. salt
1/8 t. garlic salt

2 t. Worcestershire sauce
2 c. raw pumpkin seeds, cleaned
   and dried

Combine all ingredients in a bowl; mix thoroughly. Spread on an lightly greased baking sheet. Bake at 275 degrees for one hour, or until golden, stirring every 30 minutes. Cool. Serves 3 to 4.

Fill small bags with crunchy treats
and place in a basket as
a take-home gift for guests.

Colorful Crab Appetizer Pizza
Joyceann Dreibelbis
Wooster, OH

This is a really easy-to-make appetizer that's both a fresh-tasting and lovely variation of a chilled vegetable pizza. Can be served as a snack for parties or for a light main dish with a soup or salad.

8-oz. tube refrigerated
    crescent rolls
8-oz. pkg. cream cheese,
    softened
1-1/2 c. fresh spinach, coarsely
    chopped and divided
1 green onion, thinly sliced
1 t. lemon zest, divided

1/2 t. lemon juice
1/2 t. dried dill weed
1/8 t. pepper
1-1/4 c. imitation crabmeat,
    chopped
1/4 c. chopped black olives,
    drained

Unroll crescent roll dough; place on an ungreased 12" round pizza pan. Flatten dough to form a crust, sealing seams and perforations. Bake at 350 degrees for 8 to 10 minutes, until lightly golden; cool. In a bowl, beat cream cheese until smooth. Stir in one cup spinach, onion, 1/2 teaspoon lemon zest, lemon juice and seasonings. Spread mixture over crust. Top with crabmeat, olives and remaining spinach and zest. Cover and chill; cut into bite-size squares. Serves 8 to 10.

Two sounds of autumn are unmistakable...the hurrying rustle
of crisp leaves blown along the street by a gusty wind,
and the gabble of a flock of migrating geese.
– Hal Borland

Soups & Breads
for
Chilly Days

Harvest
Homestyle Meals

Chicken Corn Chowder

Tammie McClendon
Guild, TN

Super-easy comfort food that's perfect for autumn...
great served with Mexican cornbread!

10-3/4 oz. can cream of
   chicken soup
10-3/4 oz. can cream of
   potato soup
11-oz. can sweet corn & diced
   peppers, drained
1-1/2 c. milk

1 c. chicken broth
1/3 c. green onions, chopped
2 c. cooked chicken breast,
   chopped
1-1/2 c. shredded Cheddar
   cheese

In a large saucepan over medium heat, combine soups, corn, milk, chicken broth and green onions. Add chopped chicken. Simmer until soup is almost boiling; do not allow to boil. Remove from heat. Stir in cheese; let stand for several minutes, until melted. Serves 4.

Make a tasty topping for Chicken Corn Chowder. Combine 1/2 cup sour cream and 2 tablespoons of canned chipotles in adobo sauce. Dollop over bowls of hot soup.

Soups & Breads
for *Chilly Days*

Mexican Cornbread

Arleen Collier
Owensboro, KY

My mother-in-law was a great cook. She always made
this cornbread to go with her chili.

2 eggs, beaten
1 c. sour cream
1 c. canned cream-style corn
1/2 c. oil
1 c. self-rising cornmeal
1 t. garlic powder

1 c. shredded Cheddar or Pepper
   Jack cheese
1/2 c. onion, chopped
1/4 c. jalapeño peppers, chopped
   and seeded

In a bowl, stir together eggs, sour cream, corn, oil, cornmeal and garlic powder. Fold in cheese, onion and peppers. Pour batter into a greased 9"x9" baking pan. Bake at 350 degrees for 45 to 50 minutes, until a toothpick comes out clean. Serves 6 to 8.

Bacon-Corn Chowder

Julie Owens
Freeville, NY

Perfect for a chilly autumn day!

4 potatoes, peeled and cubed
3/4 to 1 lb. bacon
1 c. onion diced
2 15-1/4 oz. cans corn, drained

2 14-3/4 oz. cans creamed corn
12-oz. can evaporated milk
8-oz. pkg. shredded Cheddar
   Jack cheese

Add potatoes to a large pot; add enough water to cover by 2 inches. Bring to a boil over high heat; cook until soft. Do not drain. Meanwhile, in a skillet over medium heat, cook bacon until extra crisp. Drain bacon on paper towels, reserving drippings. Cook onion in drippings until golden. Add onion mixture, corn and evaporated milk to soup pot; stir. Bring to a low boil, stirring occasionally. Remove from heat. Crumble bacon over soup. Add cheese; stir until melted. Serves 8.

Nothing goes better with soup than warm cornbread! Bake it
in a vintage cast-iron skillet...cornbread will bake up
with a crisp golden crust.

Farmstand Vegetable Soup

Jill Burton
Gooseberry Patch

My favorite vegetable soup! Whether I'm using up odds & ends from the last of our garden, or visiting an end-of-season farmers' market, this is how I use all those gorgeous veggies. This soup tastes even better the next day...add a basket of hot rolls and enjoy!

2 T. olive oil
2 c. onions, thinly sliced
1 c. celery, thinly sliced
2 t. Italian seasoning
salt and pepper to taste
3 14-1/2 oz. cans chicken broth
28-oz. can petite diced tomatoes

1 T. tomato paste
3 c. water
8 c. chopped or sliced vegetables
  like potatoes, carrots, corn,
  green beans, lima beans
  and peas

Heat oil in a large stockpot over medium heat. Add onions, celery and Italian seasoning; season with salt and pepper. Cook, stirring often, until onions are translucent, 5 to 8 minutes. Add chicken broth, tomatoes with juice, tomato paste and 3 cups water to pot; stir well and bring to a boil. Reduce heat to medium-low. Simmer, uncovered, for 20 minutes. Add vegetables to pot; return to a simmer. Cook, uncovered, until vegetables are tender, 20 to 25 minutes. Makes 8 servings.

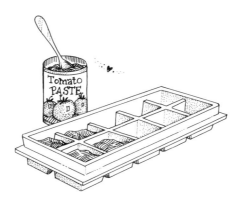

A spoonful or two of tomato paste adds rich flavor to soups and stews. If you have a partial can left over, freeze the rest in ice cube trays, then pop out and store in a freezer bag. Frozen cubes can be dropped right into simmering dishes...no need to thaw.

Soups & Breads for *Chilly Days*

Nat's Broccoli-Cheese Soup

Amy Thomason Hunt
Traphill, NC

My son Nathaniel loves broccoli-Cheddar soup. I've added a few ingredients to make it even tastier. Everyone loves it, especially Nat. Sure to warm you right down to your toes!

4 c. chicken broth
4 c. broccoli, chopped
1/2 c. carrots, peeled
   and shredded
1/2 c. onion, diced
1 clove garlic, minced
1/2 t. cayenne pepper

1/4 t. nutmeg
salt and pepper to taste
3 to 4 c. half-and-half
2 T. butter, sliced
16-oz. pkg. shredded Cheddar
   cheese

In a large soup pot over medium-high heat, combine chicken broth, broccoli, carrots, onion, garlic and seasonings. Bring to a boil. Reduce heat to medium-low; simmer for 15 minutes, stirring occasionally. Add half-and-half and butter; heat through. Add cheese and stir until melted and thoroughly combined. Makes 6 to 8 servings.

Visit a pottery studio with friends and try your hand at throwing clay soup bowls. Decorate and fire your creations to take home...even the simplest bowls will serve up fun memories along with the soup!

Butternut Squash & Apple Bisque

Suzanne Ruminski
Johnson City, NY

I first tasted a soup of this kind on a fall day while at an outdoor quilt show. I played around a bit until I came up with this. I served it to my "tea ladies," who enjoyed it!

5 c. chicken broth
3 lbs. butternut squash, peeled, seeded, and chopped
2 to 3 apples, peeled, cored and chopped
1 onion, coarsely chopped
4 cloves garlic, minced
1/2 t. dried thyme

1/8 t. dried rosemary
1/8 t. marjoram
1/4 t. white pepper
1/2 t. black pepper
1/4 c. butter
1/4 c. all-purpose flour
1-1/2 c. whipping cream
Optional: salt to taste

In a stockpot, combine chicken broth, squash, apples, onion, garlic and seasonings. Bring to a boil over high heat; reduce heat to medium-low. Simmer for 45 minutes, or until squash and apples are tender. Working in batches, purée soup in a blender or food processor; return to stockpot and keep warm. Melt butter in a small saucepan over medium heat; stir in flour until smooth. Slowly stir flour mixture into soup; whisk well. Bring to a boil; stir until thickened. Remove from heat; add cream and warm through. Season with salt, if desired. Serves 6 to 8.

Grab your camera and notebook! Autumn is a fabulous time to take a bike ride...snap some photos, gather leaves for pressing and enjoy a sky that's as blue as a robin's egg.

Tomato, Spinach & Basil Soup

Cheryl Culver
Coyle, OK

This recipe uses green leafy veggies in a delicious, healthy soup.
It's a different twist on old-fashioned tomato soup. Serve with
some crusty French bread and enjoy.

2 T. butter
1 c. yellow onion, chopped
1 t. garlic, minced
1-1/2 c. milk
28-oz. can tomato purée
1 T. sugar

2 c. fresh spinach, torn
1/4 c. fresh basil, chopped
1/2 t. salt
1 t. pepper
1 T. grated Parmesan cheese

Melt butter in a large saucepan over medium heat. Add onion and garlic; sauté for 3 minutes. Stir in milk; cook for 2 minutes, stirring occasionally. Stir in tomato purée and sugar; cover and bring to a boil over high heat. Reduce heat to low; cover and simmer for 5 minutes. Stir in spinach, basil, salt and pepper. Simmer, uncovered, for 2 minutes, stirring occasionally. Sprinkle with Parmesan cheese and serve. Makes 4 to 6 servings.

Simple Soda Biscuits

Julie Harris
Fleetwood, PA

My family loves these biscuits drizzled with honey,
or dusted with cinnamon and sugar!

4 c. biscuit baking mix
1 c. sour cream

1 c. lemon-lime soda
1/2 c. butter, melted

In a bowl, combine baking mix, sour cream and soda; stir until a sticky dough forms. Lightly flour countertop; pat dough into a 13-inch by 9-inch rectangle. With a greased knife, cut into 8 squares. Spread melted butter in a 13"x9" baking pan. Arrange squares in pan, making sure there is some butter between the biscuits. Bake at 450 degrees for 15 minutes, or until golden. Serve warm. Makes 8 biscuits.

Spicy Pork & Hominy Stew

Rita Morgan
Pueblo, CO

This hearty stew is a snap to put together. If you prefer, combine everything in your slow cooker and cook on low for four hours. I like to serve it with flour tortillas for dipping.

2 lbs. boneless pork loin,
   cut into 1/2-inch cubes
1 t. oil
1 c. onion, diced
2 cloves garlic, minced
2 15-oz. cans yellow hominy,
   drained
2 16-oz. cans cannellini
   beans, drained

10-oz. can diced tomatoes
   with green chiles
3 4-oz. cans diced green
   chiles, drained
2 T. chili powder
1 T. ground cumin
1 T. pepper
2 t. dried oregano
salt to taste

In a large Dutch oven over medium heat, brown pork cubes in oil with onion and garlic. Drain; stir in remaining ingredients except salt. Reduce heat to medium-low. Cover and simmer for one hour, stirring occasionally. Season with salt as desired. Makes 10 to 12 servings.

If you love super-spicy foods, give New Mexico chili powder a try. Sold at Hispanic and specialty food stores, it contains pure ground red chili peppers, unlike regular chili powder which is a blend of chili, garlic and other seasonings.

Soups & Breads
for *Chilly Days*

Aunt Edna's Easy Yeast Cornbread

Joanna Whelan
Mayfield, KY

Daddy's sister Edna always made everything from scratch.
She took the time to show us girls how to cook and
shared her homemade recipes with us.

3/4 c. cornmeal
1/2 c. all-purpose flour
1/2 env. instant-rise yeast
1-1/2 t. sugar
1/2 t. salt

3/4 t. baking powder
1/4 t. baking soda
1 egg, beaten
1 c. buttermilk
1/4 c. oil

In a large bowl, combine cornmeal, flour, yeast, sugar, salt, baking powder and baking soda; set aside. In a separate bowl, whisk together egg, buttermilk and oil; add to cornmeal mixture. Stir until just lightly mixed. Pour batter into a greased 8"x8" baking pan. Bake at 375 degrees for 25 to 30 minutes, until lightly golden and a knife tip comes out clean. Serves 6 to 8.

Serving soup to little eaters? Cut out Jack-o'-Lantern faces from cheese slices. After spooning soup into bowls, top servings with the cut-out shapes. How fun!

Homestyle Meals

Bob's Best Chili

Georgia Medsker
Caney, KS

This recipe was given to my husband when he worked at Collins Radio in Dallas, Texas during the late 1960s. Bob was his supervisor and he made this chili quite often. It is delicious! I have changed a few things, such as using canned pinto beans rather than preparing the dried beans by soaking overnight. Makes it easier and that makes it better, in my book! This chili is really good with a pan of cornbread, and if you have any left, it freezes beautifully.

1 lb. green peppers, coarsely chopped
1-1/2 lbs. onions, coarsely chopped
2-1/2 T. canola oil, divided
5 14-1/2 oz. cans diced tomatoes
1/2 c. fresh parsley, finely chopped
2 cloves garlic, pressed

2-1/2 lbs. ground beef
1 lb. ground lean pork
1/3 c. chili powder
2 16-oz. cans pinto beans or chili beans, drained and rinsed
1-1/2 t. cumin seed
2 T. salt
1-1/2 t. pepper

In a large soup pot over medium heat, sauté green peppers and onions in 1-1/2 tablespoons oil until tender. Stir in tomatoes with juice, parsley and garlic; set aside. In another large skillet over medium heat, sauté beef and pork in remaining oil until browned; drain. Add beef mixture to pepper mixture. Stir in chili powder; simmer for 10 minutes. Stir in beans and remaining seasonings. Cover and simmer over medium-low heat for one hour, stirring occasionally. Uncover and continue cooking for 30 minutes. Skim any fat from top before serving. Makes 4 quarts.

If you were to ask me what is most important in a home, I would say memories.
– Lillian Gish

Soups & Breads
for *Chilly Days*

3-Bean & Rice Soup

Jennifer Niemi
Nova Scotia, Canada

So satisfying when there's a chill in the air! This can be put together easily in under an hour, perhaps after a brisk walk in the chilly air. Super nutritious! This soup will thicken over time, so if you have leftovers, you'll likely want to add a little more vegetable broth, maybe even as much as another 4 cups. Serve with fresh rolls for a deliciously hearty meal.

4 c. onion, finely chopped
1/4 c. olive oil
8 c. vegetable broth
28-oz. can diced tomatoes
16-oz. can black beans, drained and rinsed
16-oz. can red kidney beans, drained and rinsed

16-oz. can white kidney beans, drained and rinsed
1 c. long-grain brown rice, uncooked
5 to 6 cloves garlic, minced
1 t. pepper
2 t. sugar

In a large soup pot or Dutch oven, cook onion in olive oil over medium heat for 10 minutes, or until soft and translucent. Stir in vegetable broth, tomatoes with juice and remaining ingredients; bring to a boil. Reduce heat to medium-low. Simmer, covered, for 35 minutes, stirring occasionally. Serves 8 to 12.

Hollow out round crusty loaves for bread bowls in a hurry...
they make hot soup even tastier!

Italian Harvest Soup

Andrea Heyart
Savannah, TX

When the weather turns chilly, I find myself standing over a simmering soup pot several nights a week. My husband and I enjoy this Italian soup with warm garlic bread for a chill-chasing dinner.

1 lb. Italian ground pork sausage
3 oz. pancetta or thick-cut bacon, diced
1 yellow onion, diced
1 stalk celery, sliced
1 t. garlic, minced
2 32-oz. containers chicken broth
10-1/2 oz. can vegetable broth
3 russet potatoes, peeled and cubed
1/3 bunch fresh kale, chopped
1/4 t. nutmeg
1/2 t. cayenne pepper
salt and pepper to taste
1 c. whipping cream

Brown sausage in a large stockpot over medium heat; drain. Add pancetta or bacon, onion and celery; sauté until tender. Add garlic and cook until golden. Add chicken and vegetable broths; bring to a low boil. Add potatoes; simmer until fork tender. Stir in remaining ingredients except cream; cover and simmer over medium-low heat for at least 20 minutes. Stir in cream. Serve warm. Makes 8 to 10 servings.

Top bowls of soup with crunchy cheese toasts. Thinly slice a baguette and brush with olive oil. Broil for 2 to 3 minutes, until golden. Turn over and sprinkle with freshly shredded Parmesan cheese; broil another 2 to 3 minutes, until cheese melts. Yum!

Soups & Breads for *Chilly Days*

One-Hour Bread Sticks

Becky Bosen
Syracuse, UT

Super-easy to whip up! I adapted this from a recipe for dinner rolls. I love to fix these when time is short. Perfect with chili, soup or your favorite pasta dish.

1-1/2 c. warm water, 110 to 115 degrees
1 T. active dry yeast
2 T. sugar
4 T. butter, softened and divided
1-1/8 t. salt
3-3/4 c. all-purpose flour, or more as needed
3 T. grated Parmesan cheese
1/8 t. garlic powder

Add warm water to a large bowl. Sprinkle yeast and sugar over water; let stand for 5 minutes. Add 2 tablespoons softened butter and salt; stir in flour, one cup at a time. Mix well. If dough is sticky, add more flour, one tablespoon at a time, until a smooth dough forms. Knead dough for 3 minutes. Cover dough with a tea towel; let stand for 20 minutes. Divide dough into 20 pieces; roll into 8-inch ropes. Arrange on parchment paper-lined baking sheets, 1/2-inch apart. Cover and let rise for 20 minutes. Melt remaining butter and brush over bread sticks; sprinkle with cheese and garlic powder. Bake at 400 degrees for 15 to 18 minutes. Makes 10 bread sticks.

Invite neighbors over for a simple meal...outside around the fire ring or inside by the fireplace. It's a great way to catch up with one another.

Chicken & Couscous Stew

Kathy Grashoff
Fort Wayne, IN

Love, love, love this recipe! You get lots of good things and it's great on those cold, cold nights. The original recipe gives you loads of chicken and it's a little thicker because of the couscous. Sometimes for just the two of us, I use 2 to 4 chicken thighs and less couscous.

3 T. olive oil
1 c. onion, sliced
1/2 c. pearled couscous,
   uncooked
4 cloves garlic, chopped
1 sprig fresh rosemary
4 c. low-sodium chicken broth

6 boneless, skinless chicken
   thighs
1/2 t. kosher salt
1/4 t. pepper
1 bunch fresh spinach, coarsely
   chopped
Garnish: grated Parmesan cheese

Heat oil in a Dutch oven over medium heat; add onion and couscous. Cook, stirring occasionally, until onion is soft and couscous is lightly golden, 8 to 10 minutes. Add garlic and rosemary sprig. Cook, stirring occasionally, until fragrant, one to 2 minutes. Discard rosemary sprig. Add chicken broth, chicken, salt and pepper; bring to a boil. Reduce heat to low. Simmer, stirring occasionally, until chicken is cooked through and couscous is tender, 15 to 20 minutes. Remove chicken and coarsely shred using 2 forks; return to pot. Stir in spinach. Serve topped with Parmesan cheese. Makes 4 servings.

Whip up a simple rustic centerpiece...fill an old-fashioned colander with colorful apples and pears. They're perfect for snacking too.

Chicken Parmesan Soup

Mia Rossi
Charlotte, NC

Our favorite Italian dish, but in a soup! My family just loves this.
I make it a meal with a tossed salad and my best garlic bread.

1 T. olive oil
1 c. onion, chopped
3 cloves garlic, minced
3 T. tomato paste
1 t. red pepper flakes
14-1/2 oz. can diced tomatoes
6 c. chicken broth
8-oz. pkg. penne pasta,
   uncooked

2 boneless, skinless chicken
   breasts, cooked and diced
1-1/2 c. shredded mozzarella
   cheese
1 c. shredded Parmesan cheese
1 T. fresh parsley, chopped
salt and pepper to taste

Heat oil in a large soup pot over medium heat. Add onion; cook and stir until soft, about 5 minutes. Add garlic and cook for one minute, or until fragrant. Stir in tomato paste and red pepper flakes. Add tomatoes with juice and chicken broth; bring to a simmer. Stir in pasta and cook until tender, 8 to 10 minutes. Add chicken, cheeses and parsley; season with salt and pepper. Let stand until cheese melts. Ladle into bowls. Serves 4 to 6.

Warm garlic bread can't be beat! Mix 1/2 cup melted butter and 2 teaspoons minced garlic; spread over a split loaf of Italian bread. Sprinkle with chopped fresh parsley. Bake at 350 degrees for 8 minutes, or until hot, then broil briefly, until golden. Cut into generous slices.

Roasted Red Pepper & Cauliflower Soup

Mary Plank
Salem, OR

I got this recipe from a friend at work. It smelled so good while she was heating it up for her lunch that I asked for the recipe. She said it was an old family recipe that she'd adapted to her family's tastes. I made a few changes myself to suit our tastes...now it's one of our favorite soups.

5 to 6 red peppers, halved
    lengthwise and tops removed
1 T. olive oil
1 c. onion, chopped
1/4 t. cayenne pepper, or more to
    taste
1 t. salt
4 c. chicken broth
1 head cauliflower, cut into
    flowerets
1 t. sugar
Garnish: favorite shredded
    cheese

Flatten peppers skin-side up on a baking sheet. Broil, watching carefully, until skins are blackened, about 10 minutes. Remove from oven and cool. Peel peppers over a bowl to collect any juices. Add peppers to bowl with juices and set aside. In a large soup pot, heat olive oil over medium heat. Add onion and seasonings; cook and stir until soft, 3 minutes. Add chicken broth and cauliflower; bring to a boil. Reduce heat to medium-low and simmer, covered, for 20 minutes. Add peppers and their juices. Cover and cook until cauliflower is tender, about 10 minutes. Purée soup in batches in a blender; return to soup pot. Stir in sugar and heat through. Serve hot; sprinkle with cheese. Makes 6 servings.

A friend who's under-the-weather will love it when you deliver a goodie basket to her door. Fill it with homemade soup and bread, a good book and pair of fuzzy slippers. Just right for beating a cold!

Soups & Breads
for *Chilly Days*

Cheddar Garlic Bread Sticks

Sara Hente
Saint Charles, MO

Fantastic with tomato soup or beef stew.

1-1/2 c. all-purpose flour
6 T. butter, softened
1 c. shredded Cheddar cheese
2-1/2 t. baking powder
1-1/2 t. salt, divided

1-1/2 T. sugar
3 T. powdered buttermilk
1 c. milk
1 t. garlic powder

In a large bowl, combine flour, butter, cheese, baking powder, one teaspoon salt, sugar and buttermilk. Mix well; stir in milk. Dough will be stiff. Knead for 2 minutes; divide dough into 16 balls. Roll each ball into a 6 to 8-inch rope. Place on a greased baking sheet; sprinkle with garlic powder and remaining salt. Bake at 450 degrees for 15 to 20 minutes, until golden. Makes 16 bread sticks.

Fill summertime windowboxes, sap buckets, even watering cans with a burst of autumn! Overflowing with Indian corn, yarrow, mini pumpkins, gourds, leaves and hedge apples, they really take on a harvest feel.

Crabmeat & Corn Soup

Ruth Hebert
Houma, LA

I don't recall where I first got this recipe, but I have been using it for years. It's a family favorite and just so delicious...enjoy!

3/4 c. onion, chopped
3 T. green onions, chopped
1 green pepper, chopped
2 stalks celery, finely chopped
1/2 c. butter
14-1/2 oz. can Italian-seasoned
    diced tomatoes
15-oz. can whole corn

14-3/4 oz. can creamed corn
1 c. half-and-half
1/2 lb. pasteurized process
    cheese, cubed
1 t. garlic powder
1 t. sweet basil
1 t. dried oregano
1 lb. crabmeat, flaked

In a large saucepan over medium heat, sauté onions, green pepper and celery in butter until tender. Add tomatoes with juice and cook for about 5 minutes. Add whole corn and cook another 5 minutes. Add creamed corn and cook for 5 minutes. Stir in half-and-half, cheese and seasonings; cook over low heat for 10 to 15 minutes, until cheese is melted. Add crabmeat and cook for another 10 to 15 minutes. Makes 6 generous servings.

Spoon hot soup into a thermos and bring it along to the high school football games...a scrumptious way to warm up at half-time! To keep the soup piping hot, preheat the thermos by filling it with hot water for about 10 minutes, then pour out the water and add the soup.

Paprika Clam Chowder

Ellen Hudson
Emmett, ID

I came up with this recipe one day when I didn't have all of the ingredients for the recipe in the cookbook. I haven't used the book recipe since! Serve with garlic cheese bread on the side.

1/4 c. onion, finely chopped	1/2 c. water
1/4 c. real bacon bits	2 c. milk
1 T. butter	1 t. salt
2 6-1/2 oz. cans minced clams	1/8 t. white pepper
2 c. potatoes, peeled and diced	1/4 t. paprika

In a soup pot over medium heat, cook onion and bacon bits in butter until onion is tender. Add juice from one can of clams (drain the remaining can). Add potatoes and water. Cover and simmer until potatoes are tender, 12 to 15 minutes. Stir in clams and remaining ingredients except paprika. Simmer over low heat for another 10 minutes, or until heated through. Serve with a sprinkle of paprika on top. Makes 4 servings.

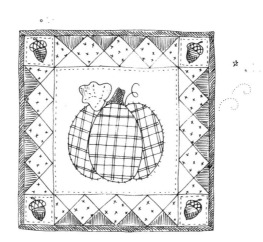

Enjoy a worn-out quilt again by turning it into a table topper.
Cut the quilt to the desired size, then stack with cotton batting
and backing fabric cut to the same size. Stitch together around the
edges and finish with extra-wide double-fold bias tape...done!

Bean & Turkey Bacon Soup

Lisa Ann Panzino-DiNunzio
Vineland, NJ

A perfect warm-you-up soup to serve on a chilly fall day!

7 slices turkey bacon
1 to 2 carrots, peeled and diced
Optional: 2 to 3 t. olive oil
2 stalks celery, chopped
1/2 c. onion, finely chopped
3 cloves garlic, minced
2 15-1/2 oz. cans Great Northern
   beans, drained and rinsed

2 c. low-sodium chicken broth
   or water
salt and pepper to taste
Optional: 1 T. fresh parsley,
   chopped

In a large saucepan over medium heat, cook bacon until crisp. Transfer bacon to a paper towel-lined plate to drain, reserving drippings in pan. Add carrots to reserved drippings along with olive oil, if needed. Cook for 3 to 4 minutes. Stir in celery, onion and garlic. Cook for 2 to 3 minutes more, until carrots are fork-tender. Add beans and broth or water. Bring to a boil; cover and reduce heat to low. Simmer for 10 minutes. Using a potato masher, partially mash bean mixture until soup thickens slightly. Stir in crumbled bacon, salt, pepper and parsley, if using. Serves 3 to 4.

Fall is the ideal time to shop for daffodils, tulips and other spring flowering bulbs! There are lots of varieties to choose from at the neighborhood garden center. Plant bulbs in October when the weather is cool.

Soups & Breads for *Chilly Days*

Fiesta Corn Chowder

Sandra Turner
Fayetteville, NC

The first time I made this soup was for a progressive dinner when my home was the "soup & salad" stop. It has become a family favorite whenever we have Mexican meals. I keep the ingredients on hand, and it only takes a few minutes to make this soup.

14-3/4 oz. can creamed corn
14-1/2 oz. can chicken broth
2 10-oz. cans diced tomatoes
   with green chiles
11-oz. can sweet corn & diced
   peppers, drained
1 lb. pasteurized process cheese,
   cubed

In a soup pot, combine all ingredients. Bring to a boil over medium-high heat, stirring frequently. Reduce heat to medium-low. Cover and simmer for 4 to 5 minutes, until cheese is melted and soup is heated through. Makes 6 servings.

Butterball Biscuits

Diane Hixon
Niceville, FL

A double dose of butter makes these biscuits flaky inside and golden outside!

1/2 c. butter, melted and divided
2 c. all-purpose flour
1 T. baking powder
1 t. salt
1/3 c. butter, softened
3/4 c. milk

Spoon one teaspoon melted butter into each of 12 muffin cups; set aside remaining melted butter. In a large bowl, sift together flour, baking powder and salt. Add softened butter; cut in with a pastry blender until mixture resembles cornmeal. Stir in milk with a fork. Fill each muffin cup nearly to the top with batter. Bake at 450 degrees for 10 minutes. Spoon one teaspoon remaining melted butter over each biscuit; bake for 10 minutes more. Makes one dozen.

An open home, an open heart, here grows a bountiful harvest.
– Judy Hand

Harvest Homestyle Meals

Terry's Garden Soup

Bernadette Seliski
Lilydale, MN

My sister Terry gave me this recipe over 25 years ago...every time
I make it I think of my "big sister" and I smile. Serve with
crusty bread and butter.

16-oz. ring Italian pork sausage
1 c. onion, chopped
1 c. celery, chopped
1 c. carrots, peeled and sliced
1 to 2 T. olive oil
2 to 3 small zucchini, sliced
1 clove garlic, minced
2 28-oz. cans whole peeled
    tomatoes
6 c. water

1 to 2 t. Italian seasoning
1 t. salt
1 t. pepper
1/4 to 1/2 t. red pepper flakes
4 c. fresh baby spinach
1/2 c. fresh parsley, chopped
1/2 c. acini de pepe pasta,
    uncooked
Garnish: shredded Parmesan
    cheese

Brown sausage in a skillet over medium-high heat; slice into rounds
and set aside. Meanwhile, in a soup pot over medium heat, sauté onion,
celery and carrots in olive oil. Add zucchini; sauté for 2 minutes. Add
garlic; cook and stir for 30 seconds. Add tomatoes with juice, sausage,
water and seasonings. Bring to a boil; reduce heat to medium-low.
Simmer for 20 to 30 minutes, just until vegetables are tender. Stir in
spinach and parsley; cook and stir for 5 minutes over medium heat. Stir
in pasta; turn off heat and cover pot for 5 minutes. To serve, ladle into
bowls; sprinkle with Parmesan cheese. Serves 8.

Gather the last of the garden veggies to enjoy throughout the winter.
Slice or cube carrots, onions, corn and squash. Combine them in
gallon-size plastic zipping bags and freeze...flavorful stews
and soups will be ready in no time!

Soups & Breads for *Chilly Days*

Savory Cheese & Onion Bread Ring

Janis Parr
Ontario, Canada

Refrigerated bread dough makes preparing this scrumptious pull-apart bread quick & easy.

3 t. poppy seed, divided
2 11-oz. tubes refrigerated
    French bread dough
1-1/4 c. shredded Cheddar
    cheese, divided

3/4 c. green onions, chopped
    and divided
5 T. butter, melted and divided

Sprinkle one teaspoon poppy seed into a greased 10" fluted tube pan; set aside. Cut each tube of dough into 20 one-inch pieces. Arrange half of dough pieces in pan; sprinkle with half of cheese, half of onions and one teaspoon poppy seed. Drizzle with half of melted butter. Repeat layers. Bake at 375 degrees for 30 to 35 minutes, until golden. Immediately turn out bread onto a wire rack; serve warm. Makes one loaf.

Cheddar Dill Bread

Gladys Kielar
Whitehouse, OH

So easy to make...great to serve with hot soup or chili!

2 c. self-rising flour
1 T. sugar
1/4 c. butter
2 t. dried dill weed

1 c. shredded sharp Cheddar
    cheese
1 egg, beaten
3/4 c. milk

In a large bowl, combine flour and sugar. Cut in butter until crumbly; stir in dill and cheese. In a small bowl, beat egg and milk; pour into flour mixture and stir just until moistened. Batter will be very thick. Spoon into a greased 9"x5" loaf pan. Bake at 350 degrees for 35 to 40 minutes, until bread tests done with a toothpick. Cool in pan for 10 minutes; remove to a wire rack. Makes one loaf.

Glazed Lemon-Zucchini Bread

Lecia Stevenson
Timberville, VA

Since I have a garden in the summer, I have an abundance of squash, so I am constantly looking for squash recipes. This has to be my favorite using zucchini...my family loves it!

2 c. cake flour	4 T. lemon juice, divided
2 t. baking powder	zest of one lemon
1/2 t. salt	1/2 c. buttermilk
2 eggs	1 c. zucchini, grated
1/2 c. canola oil	1 c. powdered sugar
1-1/2 c. sugar	1 T. milk

Mix flour, baking powder and salt in a bowl; set aside. Beat eggs in a large bowl; stir in oil and sugar until well blended. Add 2 tablespoons lemon juice, lemon zest and buttermilk; blend all together. Fold in zucchini until well mixed. Add flour mixture to zucchini mixture; stir until well combined. Pour batter into a greased 9"x5" loaf pan. Bake at 350 degrees for 40 to 45 minutes. While still warm, combine powdered sugar and remaining lemon juice in a small bowl; stir in milk until a glaze consistency forms. Spoon glaze over bread; allow glaze to set up before slicing. Makes one loaf.

Freshly grated citrus zest adds so much flavor to recipes, and it's easy to keep on hand. Whenever you use an orange, lemon or lime, just grate the peel first. Keep it frozen in an airtight container up to 2 months.

Harvest Pumpkin-Apple Bread

Sharman Hess
Asheville, NC

Truly a comforting treat with the pumpkin and apple flavors together.
An extremely moist, delicious bread. The recipe makes 2 loaves...
great for bake sales or sharing with friends and neighbors.

3 c. all-purpose flour
2 t. baking soda
1-1/2 t. salt
2 t. cinnamon
15-oz. can pumpkin
3 c. sugar

4 eggs, lightly beaten
1 c. canola oil
1/2 c. apple juice
1 baking apple, peeled, cored
    and diced

In a large bowl, combine flour, baking soda, salt and cinnamon; mix well. In another bowl, combine pumpkin, sugar, eggs, oil and apple juice; stir until just blended. Add pumpkin mixture to flour mixture; stir until moistened. Fold in apple. Spoon batter evenly into 2 greased 9"x5" loaf pans. Bake at 350 degrees for 65 to 70 minutes. Cool in pans on a wire rack; turn out and finish cooling. Makes 2 loaves.

Sweet quick breads make yummy lunchbox sandwiches. Top slices of pumpkin or banana bread with peanut butter, jam, flavored cream cheese or sliced apples. Kids will love 'em!

Santa Fe Soup

Kay Johnson
Washington, NC

This soup is always very popular when I take it to church dinners or fundraising events. A friend shared a similar recipe with me that called for ground beef. I substituted ground turkey and you cannot tell the difference.

2 lbs. ground turkey or beef
1 onion, chopped
2-oz. pkg. ranch salad
   dressing mix
2 c. water
2 15-oz. cans white
   shoepeg corn
15-1/2 oz. can black beans
15-1/2 oz. can kidney beans

15-1/2 oz. can pinto beans
14-1/2 oz. can tomatoes with
   green chiles
14-1/2 oz. can tomato wedges or
   diced tomatoes
tortilla chips
Garnish: sour cream, shredded
   Cheddar cheese, sliced green
   onions

In a stockpot over medium heat, brown turkey or beef and onion; drain. Stir in dressing mix and water. Add corn, beans and tomatoes; do not drain cans. Bring to a boil; reduce heat to low. Simmer for 2 hours, stirring occasionally. Add a little water if soup gets too thick. Serve with tortilla chips, garnished with desired toppings. Makes 15 to 20 servings.

Crunchy toppings can really add fun and flavor to soup. Some great choices...fish-shaped crackers, bacon bits, French fried onions, sunflower seeds or toasted nuts.

Ranch Biscuits

Karen McCann
Marion, OH

These golden biscuits pack in a mouthful of the zippy flavoring with the ranch taste that my family loves so well. They're wonderful served with soup, salad or even a main dish.

2 c. biscuit baking mix
4 t. ranch salad dressing mix
2/3 c. milk

2 T. butter, melted
1 t. dried parsley
1/8 t. garlic powder

In a bowl, stir together biscuit mix, dressing mix and milk until combined. Drop batter onto a greased baking sheet, 2 inches apart. Bake at 425 degrees for 10 to 15 minutes, until golden. Combine remaining ingredients in a small bowl; brush over warm biscuits. Makes 9 biscuits.

Nacho Cheeseburger Soup

Ardie Pitcher
Cavalier, DE

A great warm-up on a fall day. We like spicy food, so we add jalapeños and maybe a few slices of crisp, crumbled bacon.

4.7-oz. pkg. au gratin potato mix
10-oz. can diced tomatoes with
   green chiles
15-oz. can corn, drained
2 c. water

1 lb. ground beef
2 c. milk
2 c. pasteurized process cheese,
   cubed

In a large saucepan over medium heat, combine potatoes with sauce mix, tomatoes with juice, corn and water; mix well. Bring to a boil. Reduce heat to medium-low; cover and simmer for 15 minutes. Meanwhile, brown beef in a skillet over medium heat; drain and add to soup. Add milk and cheese; stir until cheese is melted. Serves 6.

When serving warm bread, top each slice with the prettiest butter pats.
Simply use a tiny cookie cutter to shape chilled butter slices.

Creamy Sweet Onion Soup

Tina Wright
Atlanta, GA

Delicious...pure comfort! I like to serve small bowls of this soup at the start of our Thanksgiving dinner. It reminds me of the creamed onion casserole my grandmother used to make, using her favorite onions from Vidalia, Georgia.

2 sweet onions, very finely
    chopped
1/2 c. butter
10-1/2 oz. can chicken broth
1/2 c. all-purpose flour
12-oz. can evaporated milk

1-1/2 c. water
1/2 t. dried thyme
2 bay leaves
1/2 t. salt
Optional: finely chopped peanuts

In a skillet over medium heat, sauté onions in butter until tender. In a bowl, whisk together chicken broth and flour; add to onion mixture and stir until blended. Add remaining ingredients except peanuts; stir well. Reduce heat to low; simmer for 20 minutes, stirring occasionally, until well blended. Discard bay leaves. Garnish individual bowls of soup with peanuts, if desired. Makes 6 servings.

A light, creamy soup makes an excellent appetizer before a meal.
Ladle soup into a punch bowl and surround with punch cups,
so guests can help themselves.

Walnut-Date Muffins

Gail Blain
Stockton, KS

These tasty muffins smell just like autumn as they bake.
So hearty and yummy!

3/4 c. whole-wheat flour
3/4 c. all-purpose flour
1/3 c. light brown sugar
1-3/4 t. pumpkin pie spice
1 t. baking soda
1/2 t. salt
1/2 c. milk

1/3 c. mild molasses
6 T. oil
2 eggs, beaten
1-1/4 c. walnuts, coarsely
  chopped
1 c. dates, coarsely chopped
1 T. orange zest

In a large bowl, whisk together flours, brown sugar, spice, baking soda and salt. In a separate bowl, combine milk, molasses, oil and eggs. Add milk mixture to flour mixture, stirring just until moistened. Fold in walnuts, dates and orange zest. Divide batter evenly among 12 paper-lined muffin cups. Bake at 400 degrees for 20 to 23 minutes, until a toothpick inserted in center of muffins comes out clean. Cool in pan for 5 minutes; remove to a wire rack and cool to room temperature. Makes one dozen.

For the best of the bounty, head to the pumpkin patch early! Fill a wheelbarrow with pumpkins, squash and gourds for an oh-so-simple harvest decoration. Add some fun with white Lumina pumpkins or orange-red Cinderella pumpkins.

Turkey & Black Bean Chili

Janet Sharp
Milford, OH

Our family loves chili any time of year! This chili is light,
tasty and comforting. It is a great way to add vegetables
to your family's diet...freezes well too.

1 lb. ground turkey
1 c. red onion, finely chopped
1 green pepper, chopped
1 yellow or red pepper, chopped
1 to 2 jalapeño peppers, finely
    chopped
4 cloves garlic, minced
4 T. chili powder, or to taste,
    divided

1 t. salt
1 t. pepper
15-1/2 oz. can diced tomatoes
15-1/2 oz. can black beans
1 to 2 c. vegetable broth or water
1 bay leaf
Garnish: shredded Cheddar
    cheese, sour cream, chopped
    green onions, taco chips

In a Dutch oven over medium heat, sauté turkey, onion, peppers and
garlic for about 5 minutes. Stir in one tablespoon chili powder, salt and
pepper; cook for another minute. Stir in tomatoes with juice, beans and
water or broth. Add bay leaf and remaining chili powder. Bring to a boil;
reduce heat to medium-low. Simmer for about one hour, stirring
occasionally. Discard bay leaf. Season with additional salt and pepper,
if needed. Garnish as desired. Serves 6 to 8.

Invite friends to a tailgating potluck and be sure to ask them to bring
along copies of their recipes...a super way to share game-day favorites!

Pecan Cheese Biscuits

Arleen Collier
Owensboro, KY

Our family enjoys different kinds of breads at breakfast, lunch and dinner. These delicious biscuits can be heated up for a snack too.

16-oz. pkg. shredded sharp
   Cheddar cheese
3 c. all-purpose flour
1 c. butter, softened

1/8 t. chili powder
1/8 t. Worcestershire sauce
1/2 c. chopped pecans, or more
   to taste

Combine all ingredients except pecans in a large bowl; blend together well until dough forms. Roll dough into a long roll, about 2 inches thick; wrap in plastic wrap and chill. Slice dough 1/4-inch thick; place on a lightly greased baking sheet. Top with pecans. Bake at 350 degrees for about 12 minutes. Makes about one dozen biscuits.

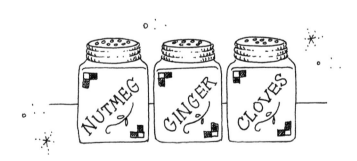

With the holidays coming, fall is an excellent time to check your spice rack. Take a pinch of each spice and crush it between your fingers. If it has a fresh, zingy scent, it's still fine to use. Toss out old-smelling spices and stock up on any that you've used up during the year.

Hearty Beef Noodle Soup

Bethi Hendrickson
Danville, PA

A great out-of-the-pantry soup that will stick to your ribs on those cold days! Serve with a dollop of sour cream or a sprinkle of Parmesan cheese and a loaf of hot, crusty bread.

2 T. butter
2 T. olive oil
1/4 c. sweet onion, finely chopped
1-1/2 to 2 lbs. beef round steak, cubed
3/4 c. all-purpose flour, divided
10 c. beef broth

2 T. Worcestershire sauce
1 to 1-1/2 c. sliced mushrooms
1/2 c. carrots, peeled and thinly sliced
1 c. reduced-fat sour cream
4 c. medium egg noodles, uncooked

In a Dutch oven over medium heat, melt butter with olive oil; add onion and cook until golden. In a large bowl, combine beef cubes and 1/2 cup flour; coat well and add to pan. Brown beef on all sides. Reduce heat to low; simmer until beef is cooked through, 15 to 20 minutes. Add beef broth, Worcestershire sauce, mushrooms and carrots. Cook until vegetables are tender. In a small bowl, combine sour cream and remaining flour; stir until smooth and well blended. Add to soup and mix well. Stir in uncooked egg noodles; cook until noodles are tender, about 10 minutes. Makes 10 to 12 servings.

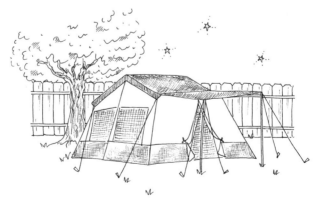

Pitch a tent in the backyard on a fall night so the kids can camp out, tell ghost stories and play flashlight tag.
What a great way to make memories!

Fresh-Picked
Salads & Sides

Autumn Pear Salad

Ginny Watson
Scranton, PA

This salad has all the good things that say fall to me! I like to use one red pear and one green one for color. Perfect for a simple lunch with warm muffins, or toss it in a bowl for a potluck dinner.

6 c. mixed salad greens
2 Anjou or Bosc pears, cored and
    thinly sliced
3-oz. container crumbled blue
    cheese
3 T. sweetened dried
    cranberries
3 T. chopped walnuts

Make Cranberry Vinaigrette; set aside. Divide greens among 6 salad plates. Top each with sliced pears, crumbled cheese, cranberries and walnuts. Drizzle with vinaigrette and serve. Serves 6.

Cranberry Vinaigrette:

1/3 c. rice vinegar
2 t. frozen cranberry juice
    concentrate
1 t. Dijon mustard
1/3 c. olive oil
salt and pepper to taste

In a small bowl, whisk together vinegar, cranberry juice and mustard. Slowly add oil; whisk until blended and thickened. Season with salt and pepper.

Create a homespun welcome...fill an old-fashioned wooden wheelbarrow with pumpkins and gourds. Add some unexpected colors by tucking in a few green and white pumpkins...how fun!

Fresh-Picked
Salads & Sides

Broccoli-Cauliflower Blue Cheese Salad

Mary Muchowicz
Elk Grove Village, IL

We love camping with our friends and always bring dishes to share along with our campfire meals. I was trying to come up with a dish that tastes good while keeping well in the cooler, so I experimented and this salad was the result. I adjust the amounts to taste, so please feel free to do so yourself.

1-1/2 c. broccoli flowerets and
   stalks, diced
1-1/2 c. cauliflower flowerets
   and stalks, diced
1 pt. grape tomatoes, halved
   or quartered
4 pearl onions or 6 green onions,
   finely chopped

10 slices bacon, crisply cooked
   and crumbled
1/2 c. chunky blue cheese
   salad dressing
Optional: salt and pepper to taste

Combine all vegetables in a salad bowl; sprinkle with crumbled bacon. Pour salad dressing over top; toss to mix well. Season with salt and pepper, if desired. Serve immediately, or cover and refrigerate until serving time. Serves 10 to 12.

A large clear glass bowl is a must for entertaining family & friends.
Serve up a tossed salad, a fruity punch or a sweet dessert trifle...even fill
it with shiny apples or colorful gourds to serve as a centerpiece.

Potato Salad with Bacon

Connie Peterson
Sunland, CA

My mom and I developed this scrumptious recipe together over the years, and I still think of her each time I make it. It is a staple at our family barbecues, and guests always love it!

6 potatoes, peeled, boiled
   and cubed
6 eggs, hard-boiled, peeled
   and diced
1 onion, minced

3 to 4 stalks celery, diced
1 lb. bacon, crisply cooked
   and crumbled
Garnish: sliced hard-boiled eggs,
   fresh parsley, paprika

Combine all ingredients except garnish in a large bowl. Add Special Dressing; toss to combine. Garnish as desired. Serve immediately, or cover and refrigerate. Makes 8 servings.

Special Dressing:

2 c. mayonnaise
5 t. sugar
2 t. mustard
2 t. pickle relish

1/4 t. celery seed
1 t. salt
1/4 t. pepper

Combine all ingredients; mix well.

Keep potato and pasta salads chilled for potlucks and carry-ins. Freeze a stoneware bowl ahead of time. Just before you set out, transfer salad into the bowl and cover with aluminum foil. This will keep the food cold longer.

Black-Eyed Pea Salad

Lisa Langston
Conroe, TX

This salad is easy and so delicious!

2 15-oz. cans black-eyed peas, drained and rinsed
1/2 c. green pepper, chopped
1/2 c. purple onion, sliced and separated into rings
2 roma tomatoes, diced

Combine all vegetables in a salad bowl. Drizzle with Balsamic Dressing; toss to mix well. Serve immediately, or cover and chill. Makes 8 servings.

Balsamic Dressing:

1/4 c. balsamic vinegar
1/4 c. olive oil
1/4 c. fresh cilantro, chopped
1 clove garlic, minced
1 t. sugar
1/8 t. pepper

Whisk together all ingredients in a small bowl.

Try this with colorful fall apples...clever photo holders! Glue a tiny clothespin to the end of a short, thin stick; let dry. Insert the opposite end of the stick into the top of an apple. Pinch clothespins open and insert photos.

Sweet and-Sour Cabbage Salad

Laura Fuller
Fort Wayne, IN

This recipe has been in the family over 40 years. It's a favorite for get-togethers and potlucks.

1 head cabbage, shredded
3/4 c. onion, thinly sliced
1/2 c. plus 1 t. sugar, divided
1/3 c. oil

1/2 c. vinegar
1/2 t. dry mustard
1/2 t. celery seed
1/2 t. salt

Place cabbage in a large bowl with a lid; arrange onion slices over cabbage. Sprinkle with 1/2 cup sugar and set aside. In a small saucepan, combine remaining sugar and other ingredients. Bring to a rolling boil over medium heat; stir until sugar dissolves. Immediately pour over cabbage mixture. Cover and refrigerate overnight, stirring after 4 hours. Serves 10 to 12.

Gather bundles of garden-fresh herbs and tie with raffia. To each bundle, add a little tag that you've written a friend's name on. A fragrant little gift and a terrific way to use the last of the herbs in your garden.

Penn Dutch Bean Salad

Arden Regnier
East Moriches, NY

This recipe was given to me over 50 years ago by a good friend and neighbor whose children I babysat. It is wonderful and always a big hit at our church's covered dish dinners.

14-1/2 oz. can French-style
   green beans, drained
15-oz. can small peas, drained
15-oz. can white shoepeg corn,
   drained
1/2 c. red pepper, diced
1/2 c. green pepper, diced
1/2 c. celery, diced
1/2 c. onion, diced
1 c. sugar
1/2 c. cider vinegar
1/3 c. oil

Combine all ingredients in a large bowl; mix well. Cover and chill for 8 hours to overnight before serving. This salad will keep well in the refrigerator up to one week. Makes 8 to 10 servings.

At your next get-together, set out a guest book! Ask everyone young and old to sign...it will become a treasured journal of the occasion.

119

Charred Greek Caesar Salad

*Irene Robinson
Cincinnati, OH*

*We love to serve this unusual salad when we grill out.
It is especially good when grilling steaks and garlic
bread...perfect for game-day dinners!*

4 romaine lettuce hearts,
   halved lengthwise

Garnish: roasted sunflower seeds

Prepare Feta Cheese Dressing; set aside. Grill lettuce over medium heat for 4 minutes, or until charred in spots, turning over halfway through. Arrange lettuce on salad plates; drizzle with dressing and sprinkle with sunflower seeds. Serve immediately. Serves 4 to 6.

Feta Cheese Dressing:

4-oz. container crumbled
   feta cheese
2/3 c. extra virgin olive oil
1/4 c. plain Greek yogurt
1/4 c. fresh dill weed, minced

3 T. lemon juice
1 clove garlic, minced
1/4 t. salt
1/4 t. pepper

Whisk together all ingredients in a bowl.

Nippy fall evenings are a fine time for a backyard cookout. Hang lanterns on the fence and in the trees for twinkling light...magical!

Fresh-Picked
Salads & Sides

Mexican Salad

Tracee Cummins
Georgetown, TX

My family has been making this salad for as long as I can remember! Its fresh taste and crisp crunch complement any backyard barbecue, picnic or tailgating party. It's also fast and easy to toss together. A definite family go-to recipe whenever we're in a hurry but need something delicious!

1 large head green leaf lettuce, torn into bite-size pieces
3 tomatoes, chopped
1 purple onion, sliced and separated into rings
16-oz. can pinto beans, drained and rinsed

2 to 3 c. shredded Cheddar cheese
5-oz. pkg. corn chips
Catalina salad dressing to taste

In a large salad bowl, toss together vegetables, beans and desired amount of cheese. Cover and refrigerate until serving time. When ready to serve, toss again. Add corn chips; drizzle with desired amount of salad dressing. Serves 10 to 12.

Serve Mexican Salad in colorful sweet peppers...perfect for a tailgating spread, and you can eat the container!

Harvest
Homestyle Meals

Turkey, Wild Rice, Cranberry & Pecan Salad

Jan Sloan
McMinnville, OR

This is a yummy way to use turkey leftovers.

3 c. wild rice, uncooked
4 to 5 c. cooked turkey, shredded
   or diced
1/2 c. sweetened dried
   cranberries
3 to 4 T. jellied cranberry sauce

2 T. lime juice
1/4 c. olive or corn oil
1/2 c. pecan pieces or halves
4 T. fresh parsley, chopped
   and divided
salt and pepper to taste

Cook rice according to package directions; spread on a baking sheet to cool quickly. In a large bowl, combine cooled rice, turkey and cranberries; set aside. In a small bowl, whisk together cranberry sauce, lime juice and oil; add to rice mixture along with pecans and 3 tablespoons parsley. Toss to mix well; season with salt and pepper. Top with remaining parsley; serve immediately. Makes 6 to 8 servings.

Head out to the apple orchard for a day of fun. The kids will love it, and you'll come home with bushels of the best-tasting apples for salads, crisps, pies and cobblers!

Fresh-Picked
Salads & Sides

Cranberry-Spinach Salad

JoAnn
Gooseberry Patch

A great salad for holiday meals! Prepare the vinaigrette dressing and the toasted almonds ahead of time. Then at serving time, it's a snap to put together the salad and serve.

1 T. butter
3/4 c. almonds, blanched
   and slivered

1 lb. fresh spinach, torn into
   bite-size piece
1 c. sweetened dried cranberries

Melt butter in a saucepan over medium heat. Add almonds; cook and stir until lightly toasted. Remove from heat; let cool. Prepare Vinaigrette ahead of time. At serving time, combine spinach, cranberries and almonds; toss to mix. Drizzle with Vinaigrette; toss again and serve. Serves 8.

Vinaigrette:

1/4 c. white wine vinegar
1/4 c. cider vinegar
1/2 c. oil
1/4 c. sugar

2 T. toasted sesame seed
1 T. poppy seed
2 t. onion, minced
1/4 t. paprika

Whisk together vinegars, oil and sugar. Stir in remaining ingredients.

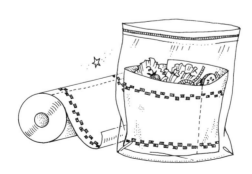

Keep salad greens farmstand-fresh for up to a week. After you bring them home, rinse greens in cool water, wrap in paper towels and slip into a plastic zipping bag with several small holes cut in it. Tuck the bag in the fridge's crisper bin...ready to serve when you are!

Grandma Nelly's Cranberry Salad

Diana Krol
Hutchinson, KS

This is my all-time favorite cranberry salad, perfect with turkey! My Grandma Nelly always made this salad for Thanksgiving. I serve it in a cut-glass bowl...so pretty and so delicious!

2 12-oz. pkgs. fresh cranberries	6-oz. pkg. orange or cranberry
1 c. sugar	gelatin mix
1/2 lb. seedless red grapes, cut in half	1 c. boiling water

Working in batches, grind cranberries with sugar in a food processor until coarsely chopped. Combine cranberries and grapes in a large bowl; set aside. In a separate bowl, combine boiling water and gelatin mix; stir until dissolved. Pour gelatin over cranberry mixture; cover and chill until set. At serving time, top salad with Pineapple Dressing, or serve dressing on the side. Serves 10.

Pineapple Dressing:

8-oz. can crushed pineapple	1 egg, beaten
1. T all-purpose flour	2 c. whipping cream

In a saucepan, stir together pineapple with juice, flour and egg. Cook over medium heat until thickened; remove from heat and cool. In a bowl, beat cream with an electric mixer on high speed until soft peaks form. Fold whipped cream into pineapple mixture; cover and chill.

If you love fresh cranberries, stock up when they're available... they'll keep, frozen, up to a year.

Fresh-Picked Salads & Sides

Quick & Easy Fruit Salad

Cindy Williams
Owensboro, KY

*This is the easiest, quickest and healthiest fruit salad recipe
you will ever find. Mix & match with your favorite fruits.*

2 Golden Delicious apples, cored
   and chopped
4 c. red and/or green seedless
   grapes

1 c. sliced strawberries,
   blueberries or raspberries
2 bananas, sliced
2 6-oz. containers peach yogurt

Combine all fruit in a serving bowl and stir in yogurt. If making in
advance, add bananas at serving time. Serve immediately or cover and
chill. Serves 6 to 8.

Ambrosia Slaw

Sue Klapper
Muskego, WI

*I love the versatility of this dish. I often change the flavor
of yogurt to match my other dishes.*

11-oz. can mandarin orange
   sections, drained
2 8-oz. cans pineapple chunks,
   drained
1 c. mini marshmallows

1/4 c. sweetened flaked coconut
1/2 c. frozen whipped topping,
   thawed
1/2 c. pineapple yogurt
3 c. cabbage, shredded

In a large bowl, combine oranges, pineapple, marshmallows and
coconut; set aside. In a small bowl, combine whipped topping and
yogurt; add to fruit mixture. Stir in cabbage. Cover and refrigerate until
serving time. Makes 8 servings.

Harvest Homestyle Meals

Pizza Pasta Salad

Amber Belt
Brookston, IN

This is our go-to potluck recipe. I like to bring something our children will eat, and they go gaga over this! If I'm bringing it to a cookout, they'll ask me to make extra to leave at home. This recipe is very forgiving, so feel free to swap out an ingredient or two.

12-oz. pkg. bowtie pasta,
   uncooked
14-1/2 oz. can petite diced
   tomatoes, drained
2/3 c. pepperoni, diced

2/3 c. salami, diced
1/2 c. shredded Parmesan cheese
1 c. shredded mozzarella cheese
1/2 to 1 c. Italian salad dressing

Cook pasta according to package directions; drain and rinse with cold water. Combine pasta and remaining ingredients in a serving bowl; toss gently until evenly mixed. Cover and refrigerate at least one hour before serving. If salad starts to get dry, add a little more salad dressing. Serves 8 to 12.

Ranch & Bacon Pasta Salad

Kim McCallie
Guyton, GA

This is my absolute favorite pasta salad. I keep all of the ingredients in my pantry and refrigerator to whip it up anytime.

8-oz. pkg. elbow or seashell
   macaroni, uncooked
1-1/2 c. mayonnaise

1 T. ranch salad dressing mix
1 T. real bacon bits
3 green onions, chopped

Cook macaroni according to package directions; drain and rinse with cold water. In a bowl, mix together mayonnaise, dressing mix, bacon bits, and green onions until well blended. Add macaroni; toss to mix well. Cover and chill if not serving right away. Serves 6.

Fresh-Picked
Salads & Sides

Tortellini Salad

Carol Patterson
Deltona, FL

A delicious variation on the traditional macaroni salad...
guaranteed to be a crowd-pleaser!

8-oz. pkg. cheese-filled tortellini, cooked
2 6-oz. jars marinated artichoke hearts, drained
1/2 bunch broccoli, coarsely chopped
1 to 2 tomatoes, coarsely chopped
1/2 c. grated Parmesan cheese
1/2 t. garlic powder
1/2 t. dried basil
8-oz. bottle Italian salad dressing

Combine all ingredients; toss well. Cover and refrigerate overnight; serve chilled. Makes 6 to 8 servings.

Cucumber Feta Salad

Jennie Gist
Gooseberry Patch

I like to serve this refreshing salad with pita chips.

1 c. crumbled feta cheese
2 T. lemon juice
pepper to taste
1 T. fresh mint, chopped
1 T. fresh dill, chopped
1 t. red onion, finely chopped
1-1/2 c. cucumber, peeled and cubed

Combine cheese, lemon juice and pepper in a bowl; partially mash cheese with a fork. Add remaining ingredients; mix well. Serve immediately, or cover and chill. Makes 4 servings.

A grandmother pretends she
doesn't know who you are
on Halloween.
– Erma Bombeck

Amarillo Squash

Jill Valentine
Jackson, TN

The men in my family don't care much for vegetables, but they love this cheesy, creamy dish! Sometimes I'll turn up the heat with jalapeño peppers and Pepper Jack cheese. It's hearty enough to stand up to tailgating burgers and ribs too.

2 t. oil
1/2 c. onion, chopped
1 lb. yellow squash, sliced
   1/4-inch thick
1 lb. zucchini, sliced 1/4-inch
   thick
1 c. sour cream
4-oz. can chopped green chiles

2-oz. jar chopped pimentos,
   drained
8-oz. pkg. shredded Mexican-
   blend cheese
1-1/2 c. nacho cheese tortilla
   chips, coarsely crushed
   and divided
paprika to taste

Heat oil in a large skillet over medium heat. Add onion and cook for 5 minutes, stirring occasionally. Add squash and zucchini; cook for 5 minutes, or until softened. Remove from heat. In a bowl, combine sour cream, chiles and pimentos; mix well and stir in cheese. Spoon half of squash mixture into a lightly greased shallow 1-1/2 quart casserole dish. Top with half of cheese mixture and half of crushed chips. Repeat layering; sprinkle with paprika. Bake, uncovered, at 350 degrees for 25 to 30 minutes, until hot and bubbly. Serves 6.

Fill vintage jelly jars with candy corn and set a tealight inside each one. Their sweet glow will make the prettiest place settings!

Fresh-Picked
Salads & Sides

Corny Popper Casserole

Cyndy DeStefano
Hermitage, PA

Corn jazzed up with jalapeños and sweet red peppers has become a family favorite side dish. It tastes great and is super-easy to make.

2 15-oz. cans corn, drained
1 red pepper, diced
2 T. jalapeño peppers, diced
1/2 c. butter, melted

1 c. whipping cream
1/2 c. milk
salt and pepper to taste

Combine all ingredients in a bowl. Mix well; transfer to a lightly greased 13"x9" baking pan. Bake, uncovered, at 375 degrees for 25 minutes. Stir before serving. Serves 6 to 8.

Candied Carrots

Tiffany Jones
Batesville, AR

My twins, Elizabeth and Noah, love these delicious carrots! They're easy enough for any meal, yet fancy enough for holiday dinners.

2 T. butter, sliced
2 T. brown sugar, packed

14-1/2 oz. can sliced carrots,
  drained

Combine all ingredients in a small saucepan over medium heat. Bring to a boil; cook and stir until brown sugar is dissolved and carrots are glazed. Makes 4 servings.

Fill windowboxes with mini pumpkins, gourds, colorful leaves and bittersweet vines...a quick & easy fall decoration that's finished in minutes.

Spinach & Artichoke Casserole

Sharon Velenosi
Costa Mesa, CA

This is a delicious side dish. I've also served it as
a main dish for my vegetarian friends. It doubles easily.

2 10-oz. pkgs. frozen chopped
  spinach, thawed
6-oz. jar marinated artichoke
  hearts, drained and
  2 T. marinade reserved
2 T. butter
1/2 c. onion, chopped

10-3/4 oz. can cream of celery or
  mushroom soup
4 eggs, beaten
3/4 t. dried oregano
1/4 t. nutmeg
1/8 t. pepper
1/4 c. grated Parmesan cheese

Squeeze all moisture from spinach; set aside. Chop artichokes; set aside.
Melt butter in a skillet over medium heat; sauté onion until translucent.
Stir in spinach, artichokes, soup, eggs and seasonings. Spoon mixture
into a greased, shallow 2-quart casserole dish. Sprinkle with Parmesan
cheese. Bake, uncovered, at 325 degrees for 35 minutes, or until hot
and bubbly. Makes 4 to 6 servings.

Whip up some birdseed bagels so the birds can enjoy breakfast as the
season turns chilly...fun for kids! Just spread peanut butter on the cut
side of a bagel and coat with birdseed. Slip a length of raffia through
the bagel's hole and hang from a tree outside your window.

Fresh-Picked
Salads & Sides

Deluxe Succotash

Elizabeth Shewell
Youngstown, OH

I got the idea for this dish while dining at a restaurant where it was featured as the side of the day. My husband and I loved it so much, I wanted to recreate it at home. I like mine better than the original!

1 lb. ground sweet Italian
   pork sausage
1/2 c. onion, diced
1 cubanelle pepper or hot red
   pepper, diced

3 cloves garlic, minced
3 ears corn, kernels removed,
   or 2-1/2 c. frozen corn
8-oz. pkg. frozen edamame
salt and pepper to taste

Brown sausage in a skillet over medium heat; do not drain. Add onion, pepper and garlic. Cook and stir until onion and peppers are tender, about 4 minutes. Stir in corn and edamame. Cover and cook for about 10 more minutes, stirring occasionally. Season with salt and pepper. Serve warm or at room temperature. Serves 4 to 6.

Autumn Hubbard Squash

Nancy Heesch
Sioux Falls, SD

My aunt used to make this recipe for Thanksgiving.

9 c. Hubbard squash, peeled,
   seeded and diced
2 pears, cored and cut into
   1-inch cubes

1 c. fresh cranberries
1 T. margarine
2 T. water

Combine all ingredients in a 3-quart casserole dish coated with non-stick vegetable spray. Cover and bake at 350 degrees for 50 minutes, or until squash is tender. Makes 10 to 12 servings.

Country Hashbrown Casserole

Becca Jones
Jackson, TN

Several years ago I was thumbing through my cookbooks and found this recipe. It has definitely been a keeper. I hope your family enjoys it as much as mine does!

26-oz. pkg. frozen country-style
    hashbrown potatoes
2 c. Colby or mild Cheddar
    cheese, shredded
1/4 c. onion, minced
1 c. milk

1/2 c. chicken broth
2 T. butter, melted
1/8 t. garlic powder
1 t. salt
1/4 t. pepper

Combine potatoes, cheese and onion in a greased 3-quart casserole dish; set aside. Combine remaining ingredients in a bowl; pour over potato mixture and stir well. Bake, uncovered, at 425 degrees for 45 to 60 minutes, until bubbly and golden. Serves 10.

Country Garlic & Herb Potatoes

James Bohner
Harrisburg, PA

These potatoes are quick & easy and you can add any herbs you like. Also, add thick slices of onion for a great side dish. In the summer, use fresh herbs from your garden for a special touch.

1/4 c. olive oil
2 T. garlic salt
2 T. dried thyme

5 russet potatoes, cut into
    wedges or slices

In a large bowl, mix together oil and seasonings. Add potatoes; toss to coat well and spread on an ungreased baking sheet. Bake at 375 for 15 to 20 minutes, until tender and golden. Serves 5.

Mash potatoes with a potato ricer or food mill...
they will come out light, fluffy and oh-so creamy!

Fresh-Picked
Salads & Sides

Delicious Scalloped Potatoes

Katy Taylor
Ontario, Canada

I used to make scalloped potatoes with my mom, and it felt like it took forever! It was an-all day event. As I grew up, I knew there had to be an easier way. So I came up with this easy recipe, and it's my absolute favorite!

10 to 12 potatoes, peeled and
    thinly sliced
1 c. onion, diced
2 T. butter
2 T. all-purpose flour

1-1/2 to 2 c. whipping cream
    or milk
2 c. shredded Cheddar cheese,
    divided
salt and pepper to taste

Set aside sliced potatoes in a bowl of cold water. In a skillet over medium heat, sauté onion in butter until softened. Sprinkle with flour and mix well. Add cream or milk. Cook, stirring constantly, until thickened, about 5 to 10 minutes. Stir in half of cheese. Drain potatoes and layer in a lightly greased 3-quart casserole dish, spooning some of cheese mixture over each layer. Cover and bake at 350 degrees for 30 to 35 minutes. Uncover; top with remaining cheese. Bake, uncovered, for another 30 to 35 minutes, until bubbly and potatoes are tender. Serves 6.

Begin a new Thanksgiving tradition. Ask your friends & family to bring a pair of warm mittens or gloves to dinner, then deliver them to your local shelter. Sure to warm hearts as well as hands!

Crustless Spinach Quiche

Shirley Lafferty
Beloit, KS

This quiche is tasty at brunch, lunch or dinner. You can bake it in a pie crust if you like, but I don't since I'm diabetic. I don't think you will miss the crust.

2 eggs, beaten
1 c. half-and-half
1/4 c. ricotta cheese
1/2 t. garlic powder
pepper to taste
9-oz. pkg. frozen chopped
    spinach, thawed and drained

1/2 c. mushrooms, chopped
2 green onions, chopped
1 c. shredded sharp Cheddar
    cheese
2 tomatoes, sliced

In a bowl, whisk together eggs, half-and-half, ricotta cheese and seasonings. Stir in remaining ingredients except tomatoes. Transfer to a buttered 9" pie plate; set pie plate on a baking sheet. Bake at 375 degrees for 35 minutes. Remove from oven; arrange sliced tomatoes on top. Bake for another 10 minutes, or until center is set. Let stand for 5 minutes; cut into wedges. Serves 4.

If you're baking a casserole at home before taking it to a potluck, keep it piping-hot by wrapping the baking pan in a layer of aluminum foil, then top with layers of newspaper.

Fresh-Picked
Salads & Sides

Creamed Kale & Gruyère Gratin

Eleanor Dionne
Beverly, MA

Kale is one of my favorite vegetables. I like to cook with it in so many different ways, from kale chips to salads and stews.

4 T. butter, divided
2 lbs. fresh kale, trimmed and
   chopped into 1/2-inch pieces
3/4 c. onion, finely chopped
2 cloves garlic, finely chopped
1-1/2 c. half-and-half

1/4 c. shredded Gruyère cheese
1/2 c. shredded Parmesan
   cheese, divided
1/8 t. nutmeg
1/8 t. cayenne pepper
salt and pepper to taste

Melt 2 tablespoons butter in a large skillet over medium heat. Add kale; cook, stirring occasionally, for about 5 minutes, until wilted. Remove kale from skillet; squeeze dry and set aside. Add remaining butter and onion to skillet; cook for 6 to 8 minutes. Add garlic; cook for one minute. Stir in half-and-half and bring to a simmer; remove from heat. Add Gruyère cheese, 1/4 cup Parmesan cheese and seasonings; cook and stir until cheese is melted. Fold in kale; transfer to a lightly greased shallow 1-1/2 quart casserole dish. Sprinkle with remaining Parmesan cheese. Bake, uncovered, at 400 degrees for 12 to 15 minutes, until bubbly and golden. Makes 8 servings.

Removing the tough stems from kale leaves is easy! Just fold each leaf in half, then cut down the side of the leaf the stem is on.

Harvest
Homestyle Meals

Honey-Glazed Bell Peppers

Andrea Heyart
Savannah, TX

These glazed peppers are delicious as a side dish. They also make a tasty topping for grilled steak, chicken and even baked potatoes.

1 T. olive oil
1 green pepper, sliced
1 red pepper, sliced
1 yellow pepper, sliced

1 yellow onion, diced
3 T. balsamic vinegar
2 T. honey
salt and pepper to taste

Add olive oil to a large skillet over medium heat. Add peppers and onion to skillet. Sauté until tender, stirring frequently to prevent burning. Add balsamic vinegar and honey; toss all ingredients together. Turn off heat; continue stirring for another 2 minutes. Season with salt and pepper as desired; serve immediately. Makes 2 to 4 servings.

Enjoy the best of the season...take a hayride, visit the apple orchard
and pumpkin patch with family & friends. End the day gathered
around a bonfire telling stories or singing songs.
Memories in the making!

Fresh-Picked
Salads & Sides

Creamed Baked Mushrooms

Michelle Powell
Valley, AL

This dish is scrumptious served over baked chicken,
egg noodles or steamed rice.

1/3 c. butter, softened
1 T. fresh parsley, chopped
1-1/2 T. all-purpose flour
1 T. Dijon mustard
1 T. onion, grated

1 t. salt
1/8 t. cayenne pepper
1/8 t. nutmeg
1 lb. sliced mushrooms, divided
1 c. whipping cream

In a bowl, blend butter, parsley, flour, mustard, onion and seasonings; set aside. Layer half of mushrooms in a lightly greased 1-1/2 quart casserole dish; dot with half of butter mixture. Add another layer of mushrooms; dot with remaining butter. Pour cream over all. Bake, uncovered, at 375 degrees for 45 minutes, or until hot and bubbly. Serves 4 to 6.

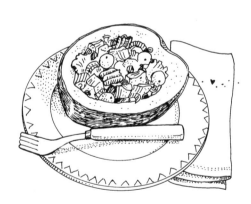

Acorn squash is a fall treat and it's easy to prepare. Place squash halves cut-side up in a microwave-safe dish. Top squash with a spoonful of brown sugar, honey or maple syrup. Add a little water to the dish, cover with plastic wrap and microwave on high for 12 to 14 minutes, until squash is very tender.

Red Cabbage & Apples

Chad Rutan
Gooseberry Patch

This easy side is perfect with roast pork, pork chops or sausage.

3 lbs. red cabbage, shredded
2 Granny Smith apples, peeled
   and chopped
1 onion, finely chopped
1/4 c. sugar

1/4 c. vinegar
1/2 c. boiling water
2 T. bacon drippings or oil
1 t. salt
pepper to taste

Combine all ingredients in a large saucepan; bring to a boil over medium-high heat. Reduce heat to medium-low. Cover and simmer for one hour, stirring occasionally. Serve warm. Serves 6.

Cinnamon Candy Applesauce

LaShelle Brown
Mulvane, KS

When my family and I went to an apple orchard for the first time, we picked 39 pounds of apples and loved every minute of it! I thought up this recipe when trying to find ways to use all the apples. My whole family loves it!

8 to 10 apples, peeled, cored and
   chopped
1 c. apple cider or water

6-oz. pkg. red cinnamon candies
1/4 to 1/2 c. sugar

Combine apples and cider or water in a large saucepan. Cover and cook over medium-low heat for 20 minutes, or until tender. Mash apples in pan with an immersion blender or potato masher. Add candies and 1/4 cup sugar. Cook, uncovered, until candies and sugar are dissolved, stirring occasionally. Simmer over low heat, mashing and stirring occasionally, to desired consistency. Add remaining sugar, if needed. Transfer to a covered container; keep refrigerated. Makes 6 pints.

To get the most flavor from dried herbs, crumble them
in your hand before adding to a dish.

Dressy Sauerkraut

Andrea Heyart
Savannah, TX

This almost-homemade recipe uses prepared sauerkraut from the deli and dresses it to the nines! Even people who don't usually like sauerkraut love this dish.

5 slices bacon
1 yellow onion, grated
1 russet potato, peeled
   and grated
2 c. deli or canned sauerkraut

1 Granny Smith apple, cored
   and grated
3/4 c. chicken broth
1 t. caraway seed

In a large skillet over medium heat, cook bacon until crisp. Drain; crumble bacon and set aside. Add onion and potato to drippings in skillet. Sauté until onion is translucent. Stir in sauerkraut, apple and chicken broth. Simmer, uncovered, over medium-low heat for 30 minutes; stir. Cover and simmer another 15 minutes. Add reserved bacon and caraway seed; toss to combine. Serve warm. Makes 6 to 8 servings.

Harvest Squash & Apples

Lea Ann Burwell
Charles Town, WV

My daughter says this dish reminds of her of autumn.

1 butternut squash, peeled and
   cubed
2 Granny Smith apples, cored
   and cubed

1 c. sweetened dried cranberries
1 c. brown sugar, packed
2 T. cinnamon
4 t. butter

Add squash, apples and cranberries to a greased 13"x9" baking dish. Sprinkle with brown sugar and cinnamon; slice butter over the top. Cover with aluminum foil. Bake at 350 degrees for 45 minutes to one hour, until squash is tender. Serves 6 to 8.

Harvest
Homestyle Meals

AJ's Sautéed Cauliflower

Angela Carter
Fairfield, OH

*My sister-in-law and I came up with this recipe one day,
and it has become a favorite.*

4 to 5 T. butter
1/2 c. sweet onion, diced
1 head cauliflower, cut into
    flowerets

salt and pepper to taste
2 T. fresh cilantro, chopped
1 T. lemon zest

Melt 4 tablespoons butter in a skillet over medium-high heat. Add onion; cook for 3 minutes. Add cauliflower; cook until tender, 10 to 15 minutes. If cauliflower is getting too dry, stir in remaining butter. Season with salt and pepper. Meanwhile, combine cilantro and lemon zest in a large bowl. Add cooked cauliflower; stir to coat. Serve warm. Serves 2 to 3.

Creamy Parmesan Spinach

Patty Flak
Erie, PA

This is the only way I'll eat creamed spinach...it's so good!

3/4 c. cream cheese
1/4 c. onion, finely chopped
2/3 c. grated Parmesan cheese
1/8 t. salt

1 t. pepper
3 10-oz. pkgs. frozen chopped
    spinach, thawed and
    squeezed dry

Combine cream cheese and onion in a saucepan over low heat. Stir until melted; stir in Parmesan cheese and seasonings. Add spinach. Cook over very low heat for 10 minutes, stirring occasionally, until heated through. Serves 6 to 8.

A delicious drizzle for steamed vegetables! Boil 1/2 cup balsamic vinegar, stirring often, until thickened. So simple and scrumptious.

140

Fresh-Picked
Salads & Sides

Spicy Garden Green Beans

Amanda Johnson
Marysville, OH

My husband loves anything spicy! These green beans are a real hit at my house. With only four ingredients, they're so easy!

1 T. red pepper flakes
salt and pepper to taste
3/4 c. yellow onion, chopped

1 lb. fresh green beans, ends trimmed and snapped

Half-fill a stockpot with water; add seasonings. Bring to a boil over high heat; add onion and beans. Reduce heat to a rolling boil. Simmer for 10 to 15 minutes, until beans are tender. Drain; transfer to a serving dish. Makes 4 servings.

Green Beans & Sour Cream

Janis Parr
Ontario, Canada

This recipe is simply delicious and a nice change from other ways of serving green beans.

2 12-oz. pkgs. frozen French-cut
    green beans
1/2 c. sliced mushrooms
2 T. butter

1/2 t. garlic salt
8-oz. container sour cream
paprika to taste

Cook green beans in as little water as possible, just until tender. Drain; transfer beans to a buttered 2-quart casserole dish. Meanwhile, in a skillet over medium heat, sauté mushrooms lightly in butter with garlic salt. Add sour cream and toss lightly with a fork; add to beans. Sprinkle with paprika. Bake, uncovered, at 350 degrees for 15 minutes, or until heated through. Serves 8.

Drop unpeeled cloves of garlic into cold water for a few minutes... the garlic will pop right out of its skin.

Julia's Squash Creole

Darlene Martin
Parkersburg, WV

A recipe created by a dear friend who passed away several years ago. Julia was a wonderful cook, a true inspiration to me...my most treasured recipes, and the ones my family asks for most often, were hers. This recipe was designed to use up the last of the vegetables in the garden.

3 tomatoes, diced
3 stalks celery, sliced
2 yellow squash, cut into chunks
2 zucchini, cut into chunks
2 medium onions, diced
1 green pepper, diced
1 red pepper, diced
Optional: 1 small hot pepper, diced

1/2 c. butter
1-1/2 c. water
3 T. sugar
1 T. dried parsley
2 t. chili powder
1 t. garlic powder or minced garlic
1/8 t. paprika

Combine all ingredients in large saucepan. Simmer over medium-low to medium heat for about 20 minutes, until mixture is saucy and cooked down. Makes 4 servings.

I cannot endure to waste anything as precious as autumn sunshine by staying in the house.
– Nathaniel Hawthorne

Fresh-Picked
Salads & Sides

Effie's Butter Bean Casserole

Susan Sparks
Kokomo, IN

This dish has been a family favorite since I was a little girl. We really looked forward to having Effie's casserole at our holiday meals! The sauce for this recipe can be made ahead of time and refrigerated or frozen, making it simple and fast if you need a quick side dish for dinner or a covered dish for a carry-in.

1/2 lb. bacon	3 c. water
1 c. onion, chopped	2 t. steak sauce
1 green pepper, chopped	1/8 t. garlic salt
1 c. brown sugar, packed	4 16-oz. cans butter beans,
2 6-oz. cans tomato paste	drained

In a large skillet over medium heat, cook bacon until crisp. Cut bacon into small pieces; return to skillet. Stir in remaining ingredients except beans. Simmer over medium-low heat for 30 minutes. Add beans to a lightly greased 13"x9" baking pan; spoon sauce over beans. Bake, uncovered, at 375 degrees for one hour, or until hot and bubbly. Serves 6 to 8.

Look for heirloom fruits & vegetables at farmers' markets...varieties that Grandma & Grandpa may have grown in their garden. These fruits and vegetables may look different, but their time-tested flavor can't be beat!

Cornbread Stuffing with Sausage

Sue Wilson
Madison Heights, VA

I fix this recipe for my family every Thanksgiving...it's always the first empty dish on the table.

1 lb. ground pork sausage
1 lb. sliced mushrooms
1 c. celery, chopped
3/4 c. onion, chopped
1/2 c. margarine

1-2/3 c. water
4 cubes chicken bouillon
16-oz. pkg. cornbread
 stuffing mix
1-1/2 t. poultry seasoning

In a large skillet over medium heat, cook sausage until browned. Drain; transfer sausage to a large bowl and set aside. In the same skillet, cook mushrooms, celery and onion in margarine until tender. Add water and bouillon; cook until bouillon is dissolved. Add mushroom mixture and remaining ingredients to sausage in bowl. Mix well and transfer to a greased 13"x9" baking pan. Bake, uncovered, at 350 degrees for 30 minutes, or until hot. Serves 8.

Serve savory baked mini pumpkins...they're so simple! Cut the tops off pumpkins and hollow out, removing all seeds. Brush the insides with olive oil; season with salt and pepper. Add a sprinkle of Parmesan cheese inside, replace the tops and bake at 350 degrees for 40 minutes.

Family Harvest
Suppers

Homestyle Meals

Spicy Chicken Spaghetti Bake

Jill Williams
Riley, KS

This recipe was given to me many years ago, and I've adjusted it to meet my family's needs. It's one of those that tastes just as good the next day as it does when you first fix it. A perfect potluck recipe too. I love those!

8-oz. pkg. spaghetti, uncooked
1/4 c. butter, melted
1 green pepper, chopped
3/4 c. onion, chopped
16-oz. pkg. pasteurized process
  cheese, cubed

14-1/2 oz. can mild or hot diced
  tomatoes with green chiles
2 10-3/4 oz. cans cream of
  chicken soup
2 10-oz. cans chicken, drained
  and shredded

Cook spaghetti according to package directions, just until tender; drain. Transfer spaghetti to a greased 13"x9" baking pan. Toss with melted butter, green pepper and onion; set aside. In a large saucepan over medium heat, combine cheese, tomatoes with juice and soup. Cook, stirring often, until cheese is melted; add chicken and mix well. Add cheese mixture to spaghetti; toss gently to mix well. Bake, uncovered, at 350 degrees for 20 to 30 minutes, until heated through. Makes 8 to 10 servings.

Have a back-to-school dinner especially for the kids. Set a table outside and serve up all their favorite foods. For dessert, build a bonfire, roast apples and make s'mores. A great way to start a new school year!

146

Family Harvest Suppers

Ron's Italian Chicken Delight

Ronald Fuhst
Summerfield, FL

This is a family favorite...we've enjoyed it for many years.

1/4 c. burgundy wine or water
2 T. butter
1 T. olive oil
1-1/2 lbs. boneless, skinless
   chicken thighs or breasts, cut
   into bite-size pieces
24-oz. jar tomato & basil
   pasta sauce

1 c. white onion, chopped
4 green peppers, sliced
1 pt. sliced mushrooms
1/2 t. dried oregano
cooked egg noodles or rice

Combine wine or water, butter and oil in a large skillet over medium heat. Add chicken; sauté until golden on all sides. Stir in remaining ingredients except noodles or rice. Reduce heat to medium-low; simmer until vegetables are tender, about 20 minutes. To serve, ladle chicken mixture over noodles or rice. Makes 4 servings.

Carve your house number into the front of a Jack-'O-Lantern,
set on the front steps and slip a lighted votive inside.
What a fun way to help guests find their way to your home!

Green Chile Baked Burritos

Danielle Stenger
Orchard, CO

I created this recipe one afternoon when I wanted burritos smothered with green chile, but did not have the time to make a batch of green chile sauce. This instantly became a family favorite! I get special requests for these burritos whenever I am having company over. It is a fairly easy dish and makes the house smell wonderful.

7-oz. pkg. Spanish rice mix
1 lb. ground beef
1-1/4 oz. pkg. taco seasoning
   mix
3/4 c. water
4-oz. can diced green chiles
16-oz. can refried beans

6 burrito-size flour tortillas
3 c. shredded Cheddar cheese,
   divided
15-oz. can green chile enchilada
   sauce
Optional: guacamole, sour cream,
   diced tomatoes, green onions

Prepare rice mix according to package directions; set aside. Meanwhile, brown beef in a skillet over medium heat; drain. Stir in taco seasoning, water and chiles. Simmer over medium heat until sauce is thickened. Reduce to low heat. Stir in beans; mix well and heat through. To each tortilla, add one cup beef mixture, 1/3 cup Spanish rice and 3 tablespoons shredded cheese. Roll up tortillas and tuck in ends; place in a lightly greased 13"x9" baking pan. Spoon enchilada sauce over burritos; top with remaining cheese. Bake, uncovered, at 375 degrees for 30 minutes, or until heated through and cheese is melted. Garnish as desired. Makes 6 servings.

Look for colorful old-fashioned cut flowers like zinnias and dwarf sunflowers at farmers' markets or even your neighborhood supermarket. Arrange a generous bunch in a tall stoneware crock for a cheery centerpiece in a jiffy.

Family Harvest Suppers

Tasty Touchdown Enchiladas

Lisa Staib
Green Cove Springs, FL

My family watches months of football each fall, and we need football food! We consider Mexican food comfort food, and I don't want to miss out on the game, so I put together a few ingredients and rejoin the game. Grab your helmets and let's go! It's easily doubled in a 13"x9" pan.

1/2 to 1 lb. ground beef
15-oz. can chili with beans
Optional: chopped onions, green
　　peppers, tomatoes
8 small or 6 large corn tortillas
10-3/4 oz. can Cheddar
　　cheese soup

1 c. shredded Cheddar or
　　Mexican-blend cheese
16-oz. can refried beans
1/4 c. sour cream

Brown beef in a skillet over medium heat; drain. Stir in chili and vegetables, if using. Spray an 8"x8" baking pan with non-vegetable stick spray. Spread a thin layer of beef mixture in the bottom of pan. Layer tortillas, tearing to fit as needed, with beef mixture and large spoonfuls of soup. Make 2 to 3 layers, ending with beef mixture. Top with shredded cheese. Cover loosely with foil. Bake at 375 degrees for 45 minutes; uncover and continue baking until cheese is bubbly. Meanwhile, heat refried beans in a saucepan over low heat. Stir in sour cream and whip by hand until very smooth. Serve enchiladas with beans on the side. Serves 2 to 4.

For potlucks and get-togethers, roll up sets of flatware in table napkins and place in a shallow tray. An easy do-ahead for the hostess...guests will find it simple to pull out individual sets too.

149

Pork Chops & Red Gravy

Cynthia Kellum
Idabel, OK

A yummy meal that's easy to prepare.

12 pork chops
lemon pepper seasoning to taste
1/4 c. olive oil
1 c. onion, chopped
3 to 4 cloves garlic, minced
3 10-oz. cans diced tomatoes
 with green chiles

2 8-oz. cans tomato sauce
2 6-oz. cans tomato paste
8-oz. bottle Italian dressing
2 c. water
1/2 to 1 c. Worcestershire sauce
cooked rice

Season pork chops with lemon pepper seasoning; set aside. Heat oil in a large deep skillet over medium heat. Working in batches, brown pork chops on both sides; remove to a plate. Sauté onion and garlic in drippings in skillet; return pork chops to skillet. In a large bowl, combine remaining ingredients except rice; spoon over pork chops. Simmer over low heat for 20 minutes. Serve pork chops and sauce from skillet over cooked rice. Serves 6, 2 pork chops each.

In the entire circle of the year there are no days so delightful
as those of a fine October, when the trees are bare to the
mild heavens, and the red leaves bestrew the road.
– Alexander Smith

Family Harvest Suppers

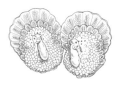

20-Minute Spaghetti

Patricia Kelley
Newcastle, OK

One of my family's favorite meals is this spaghetti, and our secret ingredient is a can of cola. We are foster parents to three girls ages eight and up, and they request this very often. I can have this meal ready in less than 30 minutes.

4 c. frozen Italian meatballs
1/2 onion, chopped
1 green pepper, chopped
1 T. oil
24-oz. jar fire-roasted tomato
  pasta sauce

8-oz. can cola
1 t. Italian seasoning
1 t. onion powder
1 t. garlic powder
Optional: 2 t. sugar
cooked spaghetti

Prepare meatballs according to package directions; set aside. In a stockpot over medium heat, sauté onion and green pepper in oil. Add meatballs and remaining ingredients except spaghetti to onion mixture. Cover and simmer over medium-low heat for 20 minutes, stirring occasionally. Serve meatballs and sauce over cooked spaghetti. Makes 6 to 8 servings.

Easy Garlic Bread

Ramona Storm
Gardner, IL

Very good served with pasta dishes and soups.

1/2 c. butter, melted
2 cloves garlic, pressed
1 t. dried basil

1/4 t. salt
12-oz. loaf Italian bread,
  cut into 12 slices

Combine melted butter, garlic, basil and salt in a small bowl. With a pastry brush, brush mixture over both sides of bread slices. Place bread on a baking sheet. Bake at 375 degrees for 13 to 15 minutes, until edges are crisp and lightly golden. Makes 12 servings.

Vintage turkey salt & pepper shakers
add cheer to any autumn tabletop.

Harvest Homestyle Meals

Sharon's One-Pot Bean Dinner

Janice Gerhart
Climax, MI

I got the basic recipe for this from my sister-in-law and adjusted it over the years. She has since passed on, so I would like to share this in her memory. My granddaughter Olivia, who doesn't like anything, absolutely loves this dish and requests it whenever she comes to visit. So it must be great!

1 lb. ground beef
1/2 lb. smoked pork sausage, sliced
1 c. onion, chopped
1/2 c. green pepper, chopped
2 15-oz. cans pork & beans
15-oz. can kidney beans
15-oz. can butter beans

15-oz. can chili beans
1 c. catsup
1/4 c. brown sugar, packed
3 T. white vinegar
1 T. smoke-flavored cooking sauce
1 t. salt
1/8 t. pepper

Brown beef in a skillet; drain and transfer to a 6-quart slow cooker. In the same skillet, brown sausage with onion and green pepper; drain and add to slow cooker. Stir in remaining ingredients; do not drain beans. Cover and cook on low setting for 6 hours. Makes 8 to 10 servings.

Bring out Mom's vintage Thanksgiving china early to get into the mood for fall. Use the bowls for soup suppers, the teacups for dessert get-togethers and even layer sandwich fixin's on the turkey platter!

Family Harvest Suppers

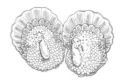

Ham, Potato & Green Bean Casserole

Carol Patterson
Deltona, FL

*I knew this recipe was a keeper the first time I tried it...
everyone had three helpings! I use boiled potatoes, but leftover
baked potatoes or frozen hashbrowns could be used too.*

6 c. potatoes, peeled, cubed
  and cooked
2 c. frozen cut green beans,
  thawed
2 c. cooked ham, cubed
8-oz. pkg. shredded Cheddar
  cheese

2 T. dried, minced onion
2-1/2 c. milk
3 T. cornstarch
2 cubes chicken bouillon
1/3 c. sour cream
1/3 c. mayonnaise

In a large bowl, combine potatoes, beans, ham, cheese and onion; set
aside. Combine milk and cornstarch in a saucepan over medium-low
heat. Cook and stir until cornstarch is dissolved and mixture is smooth.
Add bouillon cubes; cook over medium heat, stirring often, until
thickened. Transfer to bowl with potato mixture; add sour cream and
mayonnaise. Stir until well combined. Transfer mixture to a greased
13"x9" baking pan. Bake, uncovered, at 350 degrees for 45 minutes,
or until heated through. Serves 4 to 6.

Let the kids invite a new school friend or two home for dinner.
Keep it simple with a hearty casserole and a relish tray of crunchy
veggies & dip. A great way to get to know your children's playmates!

Shrimp Garlic Pasta

Amy Wrightsel
Louisville, KY

A quick & easy hit with the kids! Use sugar snap peas if you aren't a big fan of regular peas. We love it spicy, but adjust the red pepper flakes if your family prefers a milder dish.

2 c. penne pasta, uncooked
1/2 c. yellow onion, chopped
1/2 c. mushrooms, thinly sliced
2 cloves garlic, chopped
1/4 c. butter
2 c. cooked shrimp, cleaned and
  chopped

15-oz. jar garlic Alfredo sauce
14-1/2 oz. can diced tomatoes,
  well drained
1/4 c. dried parsley
2 T. red pepper flakes, or to taste
1 c. frozen green peas
salt and pepper to taste

Cook pasta according to package directions. Drain, reserving cooking water; set aside. Meanwhile, in a skillet over medium heat, sauté onion, mushrooms and garlic in butter. Add shrimp; cook for one minute. Stir in remaining ingredients; bring to a boil. If sauce is too thick, stir in a small amount of reserved cooking water, to desired thickness. Fold in cooked pasta and serve. Serves 4.

When choosing candles for the dinner table, consider how well the scent will go with food. Natural beeswax candles have an appealing mild scent...their warm amber color enhances any harvest table too.

Family Harvest Suppers

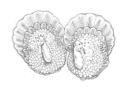

Tuna Casserole with Cheesy Garlic Biscuits

Rachel Kowasic
Valrico, FL

A quick & easy take on an old tuna casserole favorite.
The biscuits really add flavor to the whole dish!

12-oz. can tuna, drained
   and flaked
1-1/2 c. frozen mixed vegetables,
   thawed

10-3/4 oz. cream of chicken soup
2/3 c. milk
1 t. dried, minced onion

Combine all ingredients in an ungreased 11"x8" baking pan. Bake, uncovered, at 425 degrees for 20 minutes, or until hot and bubbly. Drop biscuit dough by 6 spoonfuls onto hot tuna mixture. Bake, uncovered, for 10 to 12 minutes, until biscuits are fluffy and lightly golden. Makes 4 to 6 servings.

Biscuits:

1-1/4 c. low-fat biscuit
   baking mix
1/3 c. shredded Cheddar cheese
1/2 c. milk

2 T. butter
1/2 t. seafood seasoning
1/8 t. garlic powder

Stir together all ingredients until a soft dough forms.

Mix up some fresh coleslaw in a jiffy...combine a package of shredded coleslaw mix and coleslaw dressing to taste. Stir in a drained can of mandarin oranges for a sweet twist. Perfect with fish dishes!

Harvest Homestyle Meals

Worley House Sausage & Noodles

Kelli Worley
Groveport, OH

My husband and I come from Irish and German backgrounds, both of which offer amazing foods. We like to take bits & pieces from our ethnic backgrounds and create our own memorable dishes!

2 16-oz. pkgs. Kielbasa chicken
   sausage
1 lb. fresh green beans, trimmed
1 c. water
16-oz. pkg. kluski or other egg
   noodles, uncooked

1/4 c. butter
2 t. garlic, chopped
1/2 c. sweet onion, sliced
salt and pepper to taste

Grill or broil sausage on both sides until browned. Cut into bite-size rounds. Combine green beans and water in a saucepan; place sausage on top. Cover and bring to a boil over medium-high heat. Reduce heat to medium-low; simmer, covered, for 15 to 20 minutes. Meanwhile, cook noodles according to package directions; drain and set aside. Add butter and garlic to noodle pan over medium heat. Cook until butter is melted and bubbly; add onion. Cook until onion softens. Add cooked noodles to onion mixture; stir until well coated. Season both sausage mixture and noodle mixture with salt and pepper. Serve sausage mixture over noodles. Serves 4 to 6.

ooompah!

Throw an Oktoberfest party for family & friends. Set a festive mood with polka music. Toss some brats on the grill to serve in hard rolls... don't forget the spicy mustard! Round out the menu with potato salad, homemade applesauce and German chocolate cake for dessert.

Family Harvest Suppers

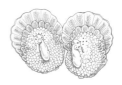

Quick Cajun Noodle Skillet

Laura Witham
Anchorage, AK

My husband and I just love Cajun cooking. Sometimes during the week, we need some comfort food to tide us over to the weekend. This is a quick, super-easy recipe I created that used everything I had in my pantry and freezer. What more could a Cajun at heart want?

1 T. extra-virgin olive oil
1/2 lb. Kielbasa pork sausage,
  diced
2 c. frozen diced okra, thawed
2 c. cooked medium salad
  shrimp, thawed

2 T. Cajun seasoning
salt and pepper to taste
4 c. beef broth
3 3-oz. pkgs. beef ramen
  noodles

Heat oil in a large skillet over medium-high heat. Add sausage and cook until browned. Add okra and shrimp; reduce heat to medium. Stir in seasonings. Meanwhile, in a large saucepan, bring beef broth to a boil. Add ramen noodles, reserving seasoning packets for another use. Cook for 3 minutes, until noodles are cooked. Transfer noodles and broth to skillet. Scrape up any browned bits in the bottom of skillet. Simmer over medium-high heat until liquid is absorbed. Remove from heat and serve immediately. Serves 4.

For a quick & easy table runner, choose seasonal cotton fabric printed with autumn leaves and Indian corn in glowing gold, orange and brown. Simply pink the edges...it will dress up the dinner table all season long!

Zesty Chicken Cacciatore

Sue Klapper
Muskego, WI

I love making this delicious meal for dinner on a busy worknight. It's so speedy, I call it Chicken Quick-a-Tore! Just 30 minutes and it is ready to serve!

8-oz. can whole tomatoes,
    cut up and juice reserved
3/4 c. sliced mushrooms
1/4 c. onion, chopped
1/4 c. green pepper, chopped
3 T. red wine or chicken broth
1 clove garlic, minced
1 t. dried oregano

1/4 t. salt
1/8 t. pepper
4 boneless, skinless chicken
    breasts
1 T. cold water
2 t. cornstarch
cooked pasta

In a skillet, combine undrained tomatoes, mushrooms, onion, green pepper, wine or broth, garlic and seasonings. Pat chicken dry; place on top of vegetable mixture. Bring to a boil over medium-high heat. Reduce heat to medium-low. Cover and simmer for about 20 minutes, until chicken is tender and no longer pink. Transfer chicken to a serving platter; keep warm. Stir together water and cornstarch; stir into vegetable mixture in skillet. Cook and stir until over medium heat thickened and bubbly. Cook and stir for 2 minutes more. To serve, spoon sauce with vegetables over chicken and pasta. Serves 4.

Start a Thanksgiving tradition! Lay a blank card on each dinner plate and invite guests to write down what they are most thankful for this year. Later, bind the cards together with a ribbon to create a sweet gratitude book.

Family Harvest Suppers

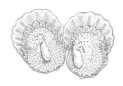

Uncle Tommy's Spaghetti Sauce

Louise Cross
Brewer, ME

You will never want another sauce recipe after you try this one! Uncle Tommy Zinni was our favorite uncle with a big booming personality. He loved the good Italian food that his mother made, and this recipe is straight from the old country. Add some meatballs and you are ready to go!

2 green peppers, diced
2 sweet onions, diced
2 T. oil
2 28-oz. cans Italian-style peeled
   whole plum tomatoes, cut up
   and juice reserved

2 12-oz. cans tomato paste
3 c. water
2 T. dried parsley
2 T. dried oregano
1/2 t. salt
1/2 t. pepper

In a stockpot over medium heat, cook peppers and onions in oil until tender. Add tomatoes with juice and remaining ingredients. Reduce heat to low. Simmer for at least 3-1/2 hours, uncovered, stirring occasionally. For the richest flavor and the thickest consistency, allow sauce to cool after cooking; flavor will be even better the next day. Reheat to serve. Makes 8 servings.

Patterned pumpkin centerpieces in no time! Stencil a favorite pattern on a white Lumina pumpkin or paint rings of white latex paint around a pale orange pumpkin to resemble a yellowware bowl.

Harvest
Homestyle Meals

Harvest Roast Chicken

Robin Hill
Rochester, NY

The first time my family & I were on our own for Thanksgiving, I was so happy to find this recipe. It's a festive one-pan dinner...just add some cranberry sauce and a pumpkin pie, and you're all set!

3-1/2 to 4-lb. roasting chicken, fat trimmed
1 t. oil
1/2 t. dried rosemary
1/2 t. dried thyme
1/2 t. garlic, minced
1 to 2 t. salt
1 to 2 t. pepper
1 lb. carrots, peeled and cut into 2-inch pieces
6 potatoes, peeled and cut into 2-inch chunks
1 onion, quartered
3 c. hot water
3 t. chicken soup base

Pat chicken dry; rub with oil and place on a rack in a roasting pan. Combine seasonings; rub 3/4 of mixture over chicken. Arrange vegetables in pan around chicken. Combine hot water and soup base; drizzle over vegetables. Sprinkle remaining seasonings over vegetables. Bake, uncovered, at 350 degrees for 1-3/4 to 2-1/2 hours, until chicken juices run clear and a meat thermometer inserted in thickest part of thigh reads 165 degrees. Baste chicken and vegetables occasionally with pan juices; cover with aluminum foil if chicken is starting to get too dark. When chicken is done, remove to a platter; cover to keep warm. Increase oven to 400 degrees; stir vegetables and bake another 10 minutes, or until tender. Carve chicken and serve with vegetables. Serves 6.

Clever placecards! Pull back the husks on mini ears of Indian corn and use a gold paint pen to write the name of each guest along the husks.

Family Harvest Suppers

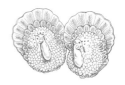

Spicy Honey-Orange Chicken

Lisa Ann Panzino-DiNunzio
Vineland, NJ

This chicken has just the right blend of spicy and sweet.

1 T. safflower oil
4 boneless, skinless chicken
    breasts
1/4 c. honey
2 T. frozen orange juice
    concentrate

1 t. orange zest
1 clove garlic, minced
1/2 t. sea salt
1/4 t. red pepper flakes

Heat oil in a large skillet over medium-high heat. Add chicken and cook for about 4 to 5 minutes, until golden. Turn chicken; cook another 4 to 5 minutes, just until cooked through and juices run clear. Combine remaining ingredients in a bowl; spoon over chicken. Cook for about 2 minutes, turning chicken to coat as sauce begins to thicken. To serve, spoon glaze over chicken. Serves 4.

Kellie's Favorite Chicken

Patricia Nau
River Grove, IL

When my daughter was growing up, this was her favorite way for me to make chicken. For a tangier taste, add more lemon juice.

1/4 c. lemon juice
1/4 c. olive oil
1 c. grated Parmesan cheese
1/2 c. biscuit baking mix

6 boneless, skinless chicken
    breasts
2 to 3 T. butter
cooked rice

In a small bowl, mix lemon juice and oil. In another bowl, mix cheese and baking mix. Dip each piece of chicken into oil mixture, then into cheese mixture. Melt butter in a large skillet over medium heat. Sauté chicken for 5 minutes; turn over and sauté until golden and chicken juices run clear. Serve with cooked rice. Serves 6.

A quick harvest side dish...stir sautéed onions and garlic and toasted walnuts into hot, cooked rice.

Southwest Quinoa-Stuffed Peppers
Helen Adams
Mabank, TX

This is one of our daughter's favorites, and we serve it with our own home-canned salsa. A perfect use for big beautiful sweet peppers from the farmers' market.

3 c. cooked quinoa
1 c. corn
1 c. canned black beans, drained and rinsed
1/2 c. canned diced tomatoes
1/2 c. roasted green chiles, chopped
1 t. garlic powder
1 t. chili powder
1 t. ground cumin
1 t. salt

1 t. pepper
1/2 t. onion powder
1/8 t. cayenne pepper
3/4 c. shredded Pepper Jack cheese
1/2 c. crumbled feta cheese
6 to 8 green peppers, tops removed
1/2 c. water
Garnish: favorite salsa

In a large bowl, combine cooked quinoa, corn, beans, tomatoes and chiles; mix well. Add seasonings; mix well. Stir in cheeses. Spoon mixture into peppers; arrange in an ungreased 9"x9" baking pan. Pour water into pan around peppers. Bake, uncovered, at 350 degrees for 30 minutes, or until peppers are tender and filling is heated through. Makes 8 servings.

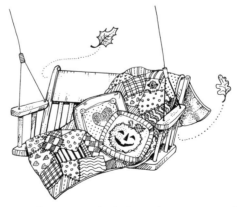

If time is tight, streamline your holiday plans...just ask your family what festive foods and traditions they cherish the most. Then focus on tried & true activities and free up time to try something new.

Family Harvest Suppers

Creamy Linguine & Zucchini Sauce
Elissa Ducar
Denton, TX

A light, meatless dinner...this recipe is a huge hit at our house! Tastes so creamy, something like an Alfredo sauce. The dish comes together quickly and the kids fuss over who gets to spiralize the zucchini! The whole family enjoys this dish, and we rarely have any leftovers.

16-oz. pkg. whole-wheat
   linguine pasta, uncooked
2 T. olive oil
2 cloves garlic, thinly sliced
1-1/2 lbs. zucchini, spiralized or
   coarsely shredded, divided
1/3 c. fat-free plain Greek yogurt

3/4 c. shredded 2% sharp
   Cheddar cheese
1/4 t. salt
1/4 t. pepper
Garnish: shredded Parmesan or
   Romano cheese

Cook pasta according to package directions, just until tender; drain. Meanwhile, heat oil in a large heavy skillet over medium-high heat. Add garlic; cook and stir until lightly golden, about 30 seconds. Add 1/4 of the zucchini. Increase heat to high; cook and stir until well coated with oil. Add remaining zucchini; cook, tossing occasionally, until tender, about 3 minutes. Turn zucchini into a large serving bowl. Add pasta and yogurt to zucchini; toss to mix. Stir in Cheddar cheese, salt and pepper. Serve immediately, topped with Parmesan or Romano cheese if desired. Serves 4 to 6.

Let everyone know what's inside each dish at the next buffet or potluck. Write each dish's name on a beautiful real or faux autumn leaf using a gold or silver metallic marker.

Herbed Roast Turkey & Gravy

Dale Duncan
Waterloo, IA

If you want a delicious roast turkey to impress the guests, this is it! Since there are fresh herbs left over, we like to tie ribbons around the table napkins and tuck in an herb sprig or two.

12 to 14-lb. whole turkey,
   thawed if frozen
3 T. extra-virgin olive oil
1 t. salt
1/2 t. pepper
1 lemon, halved
3 sprigs fresh rosemary

2 sprigs fresh thyme
2 sprigs fresh sage
2 sprigs fresh oregano
2 carrots, peeled and halved
4 stalks celery, halved
4 c. chicken broth
4 c. water

Pat turkey dry. Brush all over with oil; season all over with salt and pepper. Place turkey on a rack in a roasting pan. Place lemon halves, 2 rosemary sprigs, one thyme sprig, one sage sprig and one oregano sprig inside turkey. Arrange carrots, celery and remaining herbs in pan around turkey. Pour chicken broth and water over vegetables. Bake, uncovered, at 375 degrees for about 2 to 2-1/2 hours, until juices in thigh run clear when pierced and an instant-read meat thermometer reads 165 degrees. Baste with pan juices every 30 minutes. Remove turkey to a platter; cover and let stand for 15 minutes. Reserve pan juices for gravy; strain and discard vegetables. Slice turkey and serve with Homemade Gravy. Serves 10 to 12.

Homemade Gravy:

3/4 c. butter
3/4 c. all-purpose flour
reserved pan juices from
   roasting pan

4 c. chicken broth
salt and pepper to taste

In a large saucepan, cook butter and flour over medium heat for 3 to 4 minutes, until golden. Add pan juices and chicken broth; bring to a boil over high heat. Reduce heat to medium-low; simmer, stirring often, until thickened. Season with salt and pepper.

Family Harvest Suppers

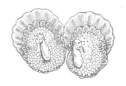

Easy Autumn Cranberry Pork Roast

Sarah Cameron
Virginia Beach, VA

Just toss all the ingredients in the slow cooker, and after a day of thrifting and garage sale-ing, you will come home to a delicious and welcoming smell. It's the taste that will really win you over! Serve with wild rice mix and veggies to complete the meal. Your whole house smells like autumn.

2-lb. boneless pork roast
2 T. French onion soup mix

14-oz. can whole-berry
   cranberry sauce

Spray a 4-quart slow cooker with non-stick vegetable spray; add pork roast. In a bowl, combine soup mix and cranberry sauce. Stir together and pour over roast. Cover and cook on low setting for about 8 hours, until roast is tender. Slice and serve. Serves 6.

Brown Sugar Pineapple Ham

Beverlee Traxler
British Columbia, Canada

A go-to meal for our family gatherings...so simple to prepare in a slow cooker, and everyone loves it. Great leftovers!

2 c. brown sugar, packed
   and divided

7 to 8-lb. cooked bone-in ham
20-oz. can pineapple tidbits

Sprinkle one cup brown sugar into a 6-quart slow cooker. Place ham in slow cooker; top with undrained pineapple. Sprinkle with remaining brown sugar. Cover and cook on low setting for 8 hours. Remove to a platter and let stand for 15 minutes; slice and serve. Makes 10 servings.

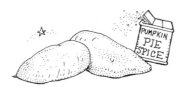

Baked sweet potatoes are an easy fall dish. Bake at 350 degrees until tender. Top with butter and cinnamon-sugar...yum!

Harvest
Homestyle Meals

Turkey & Polenta Casserole

Eleanor Dionne
Beverly, MA

This is an old-time family favorite. Try it with chicken too!

6 c. water
1 t. salt
1/2 c. yellow cornmeal
3 T. butter
3 c. cooked turkey, diced

1 lb. sliced mushrooms
2 to 2-1/2 c. meatless pasta
   sauce
3/4 c. grated Parmesan cheese
pepper to taste

Combine water and salt in a large saucepan over high heat; bring to a boil. Gradually add cornmeal, stirring constantly with a wooden spoon. Cook over medium-low heat for about 30 minutes, to the consistency of mashed potatoes. Meanwhile, in a skillet over medium heat, sauté mushrooms in butter. Transfer cornmeal mixture to a buttered 10"x10" baking pan; level off with spoon. Spoon turkey and mushrooms over top; spread pasta sauce over all. Sprinkle with cheese and a little pepper. Bake, uncovered, at 350 degrees for 45 minutes, or until heated through. Serves 6 to 8.

Turkey & Stuffing Bake

Jo Ann Belovitch
Stratford, CT

This is delicious made with leftovers from Thanksgiving dinner, too.

6-oz. pkg. turkey-flavored
   stuffing mix
8-oz. can jellied cranberry sauce

12-oz. can turkey, drained
10-oz. can turkey gravy

Prepare stuffing according to package directions. Add cranberry sauce; mix well and set aside. Layer turkey in a buttered 2-quart casserole dish; top with stuffing mixture and gravy. Bake, uncovered, at 375 degrees for 15 to 20 minutes, until hot and bubbly. Serves 3 to 4.

Host a post-holiday potluck with friends, the weekend after Turkey Day! Everyone can bring their favorite "leftovers" concoctions and relax together.

Family Harvest Suppers

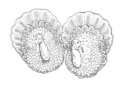

Turkey-Potato Pie

Maegan Stauffer
Findlay, OH

A great autumn twist on a traditional shepherd's pie.
A good way to use leftovers too!

4 potatoes, peeled and quartered
1/4 c. milk
1/4 c. plus 2 t. butter
1 stalk celery, sliced
1 c. frozen green beans, thawed

4 c. cooked turkey, diced or
   shredded
10-oz. can brown gravy
   with onions
6 slices Colby Jack cheese

Cover potatoes with water in a large saucepan. Bring to a boil over high heat; cook for about 15 minutes, until tender. Drain and mash with milk and 1/4 cup butter. Meanwhile, in a small skillet over medium heat, sauté celery in remaining butter. To assemble, spread beans evenly in a lightly greased 13"x9" baking pan; cover with turkey. Pour gravy over all; top with celery. Spread mashed potatoes over top. Bake, uncovered, at 375 degrees for 40 minutes, or until heated through. Arrange cheese slices evenly on top; continue to bake for 5 minutes. Makes 8 servings.

Shopping for a turkey? Allow about one pound per person plus
a little extra for leftovers. For example, a 15-pound turkey would
serve 12 people with enough left to enjoy turkey sandwiches,
turkey tetrazzini or turkey soup later.

Harvest
Homestyle Meals

Simple & Delicious Chicken Lasagna

Lacey Lucas
New Brunswick, Canada

This recipe makes two 8"x8" pans of lasagna...might as well make two at once, and freeze one for a busy night! I use low-fat versions of the ingredients to make this a little more friendly to the waistline. Serve with garlic toast and Caesar salad.

12-oz. pkg. lasagna noodles, uncooked
3 c. broccoli, chopped
1-1/2 c. red pepper, chopped
2 15-oz. jars Alfredo sauce
10-3/4 oz. can cream of chicken soup
1 c. cottage cheese
4 cooked chicken breasts, chopped
16-oz. pkg. shredded mozzarella cheese

Cook noodles according to package directions, just until tender; drain. Meanwhile, bring a saucepan of water to a boil over high heat. Add broccoli and red pepper; boil for 3 minutes. Drain; remove to a bowl of ice water to cool, then drain again and set aside. Combine Alfredo sauce, soup and cottage cheese in a bowl. Grease two 8"x8" baking pans. Spread one cup of sauce into each; add 3 noodles to each, slightly overlapping. Top each with 1/4 of chicken and 1/4 of broccoli mixture. Add one cup of sauce to each pan; sprinkle with a little cheese. Repeat layering, starting with noodles. End with a third layer of noodles, remaining sauce and remaining cheese. Cover both pans with aluminum foil; freeze one pan for later. Bake remaining pan at 350 degrees for one hour. Uncover; broil until cheese is golden. Let stand before serving. To bake the frozen pan, thaw overnight in the refrigerator, then bake as directed. Makes 2 pans; each serves 4 to 6.

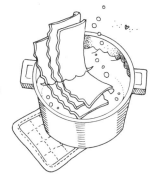

For a quick way to "cook" lasagna noodles, put them in a pan of very hot water while mixing up the rest of the recipe. They will be soft and pliable when you're ready for them!

168

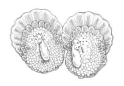
Best Baked Spaghetti Ever

Crystal Shook
Catawba, IN

Everyone loves this dish! Pop some garlic bread in the oven alongside the casserole. Toss a salad and dinner is served.

16-oz. pkg. spaghetti, uncooked
1 to 2 t. olive oil
1 lb. Italian ground pork sausage
1/2 c. onion, chopped
16-oz. jar spaghetti sauce

8-oz. pkg. cream cheese, softened
1 c. ricotta cheese
1/4 c. sour cream
8-oz. pkg. shredded mozzarella cheese

Cook spaghetti according to package directions; drain. Drizzle with olive oil and set aside. Meanwhile, in a skillet over medium heat, brown sausage with onion until no longer pink; drain. Stir in spaghetti sauce and set aside. In a large bowl, combine cream cheese, ricotta cheese and sour cream. Beat with an electric mixer on medium speed until blended; set aside. To assemble, layer half of spaghetti in a greased 13"x9" baking pan. Top with cream cheese mixture and remaining spaghetti. Spread sauce mixture over top; sprinkle with mozzarella cheese. Bake, uncovered, at 350 degrees for 40 to 45 minutes, until bubbly and cheese is melted. Makes 8 to 10 servings.

Host a family reunion this fall...the weather is almost always picture-perfect! When sending invitations, be sure to encourage everyone to bring recipes, photos, videos, scrapbooks and anything that inspires memories.

ℋ𝒶𝓇𝓋𝑒𝓈𝓉
Homestyle Meals

Harvest Grains Chicken Stir-Fry

Sandy Churchill
West Bridgewater, MA

Lately, we have been on a high-fiber kick and enjoying a healthier menu with some creative cooking. This recipe is a new favorite and features a colorful mix of grains, nuts and fruit.

1 c. quinoa, uncooked
1 c. frozen edamame, thawed
1/2 c. jasmine rice, uncooked
1 zucchini, cut into 1/2-inch
   pieces
1 stalk celery, cut into
   1/2-inch pieces
1-1/2 c. water

1 t. garlic, minced
1 t. garlic salt
1 to 2 cooked chicken breasts,
   cut into 1-inch cubes
1/2 c. frozen corn, thawed
2 T. whole cashews
2 T. sweetened dried cranberries

In a stockpot, combine quinoa, edamame, rice, zucchini, celery, water, garlic and garlic salt. Bring to a boil over medium heat; cook for 10 to 15 minutes, until grains soften. Stir in remaining ingredients. Cook another 5 minutes, to allow flavors to blend. Stir well and serve. Makes 8 to 10 servings.

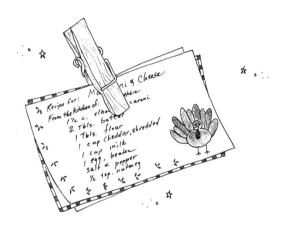

Pick up a bunch of clip-style clothespins...just right in the kitchen as "chip clips." They come in handy for clipping together recipes or coupons too.

Family Harvest Suppers

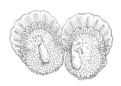

Cider-Glazed Chicken & Sweet Potatoes

John Alexander
New Britain, CT

A cozy dinner perfect for a chilly autumn evening with friends.

1 to 2 sweet potatoes, peeled
   and cubed
2 tart apples, cored and sliced
1 T. fresh rosemary, chopped
salt and pepper to taste
2 T. olive oil, divided

6 chicken thighs, trimmed
2/3 c. apple cider
2 T. honey
1 T. grainy mustard
1 T. butter
3 sprigs fresh rosemary

Combine potatoes, apples and chopped rosemary in a bowl; season with salt and pepper. Drizzle with one tablespoon oil; toss until combined and set aside. Heat remaining oil in a large cast-iron skillet over medium-high heat. Add chicken, skin-side down. Cook for 3 to 5 minutes, until golden. Remove chicken to a plate. Stir cider, honey and mustard into drippings in skillet. Bring almost to a boil; cook until mixture has cooked down slightly. Whisk in butter. Return chicken to skillet, skin-side up. Spoon potato mixture around chicken; add rosemary sprigs to skillet. Transfer skillet to oven. Bake, uncovered, at 425 degrees for about 20 minutes, until chicken is cooked through and potatoes are tender. If potatoes need longer to cook, transfer chicken to a platter; let stand. Return skillet to oven until potatoes are tender. Serve chicken and potato mixture topped with sauce from skillet. Makes 6 servings.

Hang a garland indoors this Thanksgiving...snip photos of family, friends, pets, anything you're thankful for. Clipped to a ribbon with mini clothespins, they're a heartfelt reminder to count your blessings.

Harvest Homestyle Meals

Marinated Pot Roast

Mandy Bird
Tremonton, UT

I first tasted this delectable slow-cooked roast at a wedding reception. Years later, I finally found the recipe and made it myself. It's the best roast I've ever tasted! Perfect for Sunday dinner as it can cook overnight. The drippings make a wonderful gravy.

2 to 4-lb. beef chuck roast
2-1/2 c. water, divided
6-oz. can frozen apple juice
  concentrate, thawed
1/2 c. soy sauce
1/4 c. oil
3/4 c. onion, chopped
1 t. garlic, minced
1/2 t. ground ginger
1/4 t. pepper
2 bay leaves
1/4 c. cornstarch
mashed potatoes

Place chuck roast in a 4 to 6-quart slow cooker; set aside. Whisk together 2 cups water and remaining ingredients except cornstarch and potatoes; pour over roast. Cover and cook on low setting for 12 to 14 hours. Remove roast to a platter; cover to keep warm. Pour drippings into a saucepan over medium heat; discard bay leaves. Bring to a simmer. Combine remaining water and cornstarch; stir into drippings. Cook and stir until thickened. Serve gravy over roast and mashed potatoes. Makes 6 to 8 servings.

Braised Beef Short Ribs

Sarah Oravecz
Gooseberry Patch

Your family will love these tender, luscious ribs...mine does!

5 lbs. beef short ribs
1 onion, cut into thin wedges
14-oz. can beef broth
12-oz. can regular or non-
  alcoholic dark beer
1/4 c. dark molasses
2 T. balsamic vinegar
1 t. dried thyme
1 t. hot pepper sauce
1/2 t. salt

Place short ribs and onion in a 6-quart slow cooker. Whisk together remaining ingredients; pour over ribs. Cover and cook on low setting for 10 to 12 hours, or on high setting for 5-1/2 to 6 hours. With a slotted spoon, transfer ribs to a platter; cover to keep warm. Skim fat from juices in slow cooker; serve with ribs. Makes 6 servings.

Family Harvest Suppers

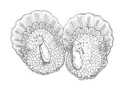

Perfect Yeast Rolls

Vickie Wiseman
Liberty Twp., OH

This is my daughter Bithia's favorite recipe. She makes these rolls every Thanksgiving, Christmas and Easter. They take a little time, but much of it is spent just waiting for the dough to rise. Everyone enjoys them, especially with honey butter.

2 T. active dry yeast
1/2 c. plus 1/2 t. sugar, divided
1-1/2 c. warm water, about
    110 to 115 degrees, divided
1/2 c. shortening

3 eggs, beaten
5 c. all-purpose flour
2 t. salt
Garnish: melted butter

Dissolve yeast and 1/2 teaspoon sugar in 1/2 cup warm water; set aside. In a large bowl, blend shortening and remaining sugar. Add eggs, remaining water and yeast mixture. Beat with an electric mixer on high speed until well mixed. In another bowl, sift together flour and salt; beat into shortening mixture in 3 batches. Continue beating until glossy in texture; dough will be sticky. Do not add additional flour. Cover and set bowl in a warm place; let rise for one hour. Punch down dough; cover bowl with a large plastic zipping bag sprayed inside with non-stick vegetable spray. Secure bag; refrigerate dough overnight. Dough will continue to rise, so make sure bag is large enough to allow for rising. (If preferred, divide dough between 2 bowls and 2 bags.) About 2 hours before baking time, remove dough from refrigerator; shape into 3 to 5 dozen balls. Arrange rolls in greased 13"x9" baking pans, rolls touching. Brush rolls with melted butter; let rise until double. Bake at 350 degrees for 15 to 20 minutes. Makes 3 to 5 dozen.

Savory smells were in the air. On the crane hung steaming kettles,
and down among the red embers copper saucepans simmered,
all suggestive of some approaching feast.
– Louisa May Alcott

Harvest Homestyle Meals

Tom's Best-Ever Salmon Patties

Thomas Hiegel
Union City, OH

I decided I wanted to eat more fish and less beef, but didn't want any fishy taste. These tasty patties are what I came up with.

15-1/2 oz. can wild pink
    salmon, drained
1/2 c. sweet onion, chopped
1/4 c. celery, chopped
2 T. butter, divided
12 saltine crackers, finely
    crushed

1/4 c. buttermilk
2 eggs, beaten
1 T. lemon juice
1/2 t. white pepper
Optional: 2 T. prepared
    horseradish

Discard any skin from salmon; add salmon to a large bowl and set aside. In a skillet over medium heat, sauté onion and celery in one tablespoon butter for 4 to 5 minutes, until tender. Add onion mixture and remaining ingredients except butter to salmon in bowl; mix well and shape into 8 patties. Melt remaining butter in same skillet over medium heat; carefully add salmon patties. Cook on both sides until golden. Makes 8 servings.

Stock up on favorite pantry items like vegetables, pasta, rice and canned chicken and tuna. They're so handy for busy-day meals in a hurry, and you won't have to go out when the weather is dreary.

Family Harvest
Suppers

Cheesy Tuna Mac

Jill Ross
Pickerington, OH

A simple dinner for a busy school night...the whole family loves it!
I doubled the tuna to make this dish extra satisfying.

7-1/4 oz. box macaroni &
　cheese mix
10-3/4 oz. can cream of
　celery soup
2　6-oz. cans tuna, drained
　and flaked

1/2 c. milk
1 c. shredded Cheddar cheese
Optional: snipped fresh
　parsley

Prepare macaroni & cheese mix according to package directions.
Stir in soup, tuna and milk; mix well and transfer to a greased 2-quart
casserole dish. Sprinkle with cheese and parsley, if desired. Bake,
uncovered, at 350 degrees for 20 to 25 minutes, until heated through
and cheese is melted. Makes 4 servings.

Give favorite pasta recipes a twist for fall...pick up some pasta
in seasonal shapes like autumn leaves, pumpkins or turkeys!
Some even come in veggie colors like orange, red or green.

Bake-All-Day Barbecue Beef

Joyce Roebuck
Jacksonville, TX

I'm 81 and I have been cooking all my life. Every Sunday after church, all of my family (and whoever else shows up!) comes to eat lunch at my house. The more the merrier! This recipe is great when you have a busy day ahead and don't want to spend a lot of time in the kitchen. With chips and drinks, it's a meal!

5 to 6-lb. beef chuck roast
1 c. onion, finely chopped
1 clove garlic, minced
4 c. ginger ale
3 c. catsup
2 T. Worcestershire sauce

1 T. white vinegar
1 t. salt
1/2 t. pepper
1/2 t. dry mustard
1/8 t. lemon juice
12 hamburger buns, split

Place roast in a large Dutch oven. In a large bowl, whisk together remaining ingredients except buns; spoon over roast. Cover and bake at 300 degrees for 6 to 8 hours, until roast is tender. May also be cooked in a slow cooker on low setting for 10 to 12 hours. Shred roast with 2 forks; serve beef on buns. Serves 12.

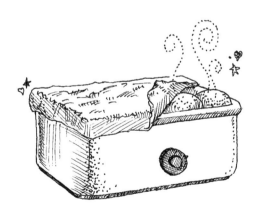

Warm sandwich buns for a crowd...easy! Fill a roaster with buns, cover with heavy-duty aluminum foil and cut several slits in the foil. Top with several dampened paper towels and tightly cover with more foil. Bake at 250 degrees for 20 minutes. Rolls will be hot and steamy.

Family Harvest Suppers

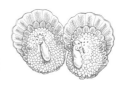

Yum Burgers

Jane Bean
LaVista, NE

*We have loved these since I was little. They're often requested
even today. We have served them at team suppers and
at my granddaughter's graduation. Yum!*

1 lb. ground beef
2 green onions, chopped
1 clove garlic, diced
1 t. dried parsley
salt and pepper to taste
10-3/4 oz. can chicken
    gumbo soup

1/4 c. catsup
1 t. mustard
6 to 8 hamburger buns, split
    and toasted
Garnish: cheese slices, pickles

In a skillet over medium heat, brown beef with onions, garlic and
parsley. Drain; season with salt and pepper. Stir in soup, catsup and
mustard. Simmer over low heat for one hour, stirring occasionally. To
serve, scoop beef mixture onto toasted hamburger buns; add favorite
toppings. Makes 6 to 8 servings.

If you're traveling "over the river and through the woods" for
Thanksgiving, make a trip bag for each of the kids...a special tote bag
that's filled with favorite small toys, puzzles and other fun stuff,
reserved just for road trips. The miles are sure to speed by much faster!

Jaclyn's Stromboli

Emilie Britton
New Bremen, OH

My daughter-in-law Jaclyn shared this recipe. It's a favorite that is fun and filling...perfect for tailgating parties and for busy weeknight meals as well.

1 loaf frozen bread, thawed
1 lb. sliced mushrooms
1/2 c. onion, chopped
2 T. butter
1/4 lb. deli baked ham, very thinly sliced
1/4 lb. sliced Swiss cheese
1/4 lb. sliced mozzarella cheese
1/4 lb. sliced provolone cheese
1/4 lb. deli pepperoni, very thinly sliced
1/4 lb. deli hard salami, very thinly sliced
melted butter to taste
Italian seasoning to taste

On a greased baking sheet, press dough into a rectangle, 20 inches long by 8 inches wide; set aside. In a skillet over medium heat, sauté mushrooms and onion in butter until tender; set aside. Layer ham, cheeses, pepperoni and salami down the center of dough. Spoon mushroom mixture evenly over top. Fold one side of dough over the other side; pinch to seal. Brush with melted butter; sprinkle with Italian seasoning. Bake at 350 degrees for 30 minutes, or until dough is golden and cheeses are melted. Let stand several minutes; slice to serve. Makes 4 servings.

Wrap a warm stromboli in aluminum foil and tuck in a basket with mini bags of potato chips, a couple of frosty sodas and a giant dill pickle from the deli...all you need for a tasty autumn picnic!

Family Harvest Suppers

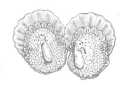

Picnic French Loaf

Nannette Scarborough
Farmerville, LA

This sandwich is a great traveler. It has always been a favorite for a day fishing at the lake or a family get-together. It is good warm or cold, and everyone always comes back for more!

1 large loaf French bread
1 lb. ground beef
1/4 c. yellow onion, chopped
1-1/4 oz. pkg taco seasoning mix

3/4 c. water
10-3/4 oz. can fiesta nacho
 cheese soup

Cut bread loaf in half lengthwise. Pull out bread from the center of both halves. Reserve bread pieces; set aside. In a skillet over medium heat, brown beef with onion; drain. Stir in taco seasoning and water; simmer for several minutes. Add soup and reserved bread pieces to skillet; simmer until warmed through. Place bottom half of loaf on an aluminum foil-lined baking sheet. Spoon all of beef mixture into center of loaf; add top of loaf. Wrap entire loaf in aluminum foil; place on baking sheet. Bake at 350 degrees for 30 minutes. Slice immediately, or let cool slightly before slicing. Makes 8 servings.

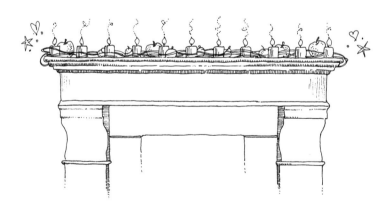

Set an autumn mood...line the mantel with lots of votives tucked inside orange, gold, brown and green votive holders. Surround them with apples, acorns and bittersweet vines. So pretty!

179

Thanksgiving Leftovers Pizza

Matthew Evans
Belding, MI

One Thanksgiving, we were tired of the same old leftover turkey sandwiches. So I decided to try something new. I decided I was going to create a Thanksgiving leftovers pizza. Now every year, my family looks forward more to the leftovers than to the actual Thanksgiving dinner! This is a basic recipe...feel free to add other leftover ingredients like cranberries. Have fun and experiment with different combinations until you find the right leftovers pizza taste for your family.

2 6-1/2 oz. pkgs. pizza crust mix
8-oz. pkg. cream cheese, room
    temperature
1/2 t. poultry seasoning
1/2 t. salt
1/2 t. pepper

2 c. cooked turkey, chopped
3 c. leftover stuffing, or as
    desired
8-oz. pkg. shredded sharp
    Cheddar cheese

Prepare pizza crust mixes according to package instructions. Spray a 14"x11" jelly-roll pan with non-stick vegetable spray. Knead and spread dough until it is spread evenly over the pan. Spread cream cheese evenly over dough; sprinkle with seasonings. Spread turkey and stuffing over dough; sprinkle with cheese. Bake at 400 degrees for 20 minutes, or until crust is golden and cheese has melted. Remove from oven; let stand for 5 minutes before slicing. Serves 10 to 12.

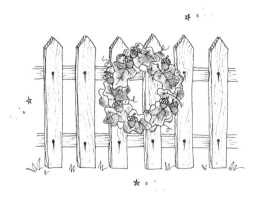

And all at once, summer collapsed into fall.
– Oscar Wilde

Cookies, Cakes and Pies...
Oh My!

Homestyle Meals

Butterscotch Zucchini Bars

Emilie Britton
New Bremen, OH

This year I started a new tradition for our family...I hosted a back-to-school party! The 12 grandkids played yard games, and everyone brought a covered dish to share. I supplied fried chicken for the main course and an assortment of desserts. These butterscotch bars were a hit! I'll make these again for next year's party as I'm already writing down plans. It's the perfect time of year to use the abundance of zucchini.

3 eggs, beaten
2/3 c. oil
2 c. sugar
2 t. vanilla extract
2-1/2 c. all-purpose flour
1 t. baking powder

1 t. baking soda
1 t. salt
2 c. zucchini, shredded
1 c. butterscotch baking chips
1/2 c. brown sugar, packed

In a large bowl, beat together eggs, oil, sugar and vanilla. Add flour, baking powder, baking soda and salt; mix well. Fold in zucchini. Pour batter into a greased 15"x10" jelly-roll pan; set aside. Combine butterscotch chips and brown sugar in a bowl; mix well and sprinkle over batter. Bake at 350 degrees for 30 minutes, or until a toothpick comes out clean. Cool; cut into bars. Makes 2 dozen.

For perfectly cut brownies or bars, refrigerate them in the pan
for about an hour after baking. Cut them with a plastic knife
for a clean cut every time!

Cookies, Cakes and Pies... *Oh My!*

PTA Chocolate Chip Cookies

Carol Hix
Mabelvale, AR

This recipe was given to me 25 years ago by a friend in the PTA group at my children's elementary school. These chewy cookies are still my favorite and my most-requested recipe.

1 c. butter-flavored shortening
1 c. sugar
1/2 c. brown sugar, packed
2 eggs, beaten
2 t. vanilla extract

2-1/4 c. all-purpose flour
1 t. baking soda
1 t. salt
2 c. semi-sweet chocolate chips
Optional: 1/2 c. chopped nuts

In a large bowl, blend together shortening and sugars; stir in eggs and vanilla. Blend in flour, baking soda and salt. Fold in chocolate chips and nuts, if using. Drop dough by tablespoonfuls onto parchment paper-lined baking sheets. Bake at 350 degrees for 10 to 12 minutes, until lightly golden; do not overbake. Remove cookies to a wire rack; cool. Makes about 2 dozen.

Making dessert for a crowd? It's tricky to successfully double or triple recipe ingredients for cakes or cookies. Instead, choose a recipe that feeds a bunch, or prepare several batches of a single recipe until you have the quantity you need.

Nona's Frosty Apple Bites

Jennifer Fox
Fredericktown, OH

This recipe is one of the few that I have in my late grandmother's handwriting. I cherish the recipe for that reason, and love the cookies almost as much as I loved her!

1/4 c. margarine
1 c. brown sugar, packed
1 egg, beaten
5-oz. can evaporated milk
1 t. vanilla extract
1/4 t. nutmeg

1/2 t. salt
2 c. all-purpose flour
1/2 t. baking soda
1 c. apple, peeled, cored and
  finely chopped
1/2 c. butterscotch baking chips

In a large bowl, blend margarine, brown sugar and egg until smooth. Add evaporated milk, vanilla, nutmeg and salt. Beat with an electric mixer on medium speed for 2 minutes, until creamy. Add flour and baking soda; beat for 2 minutes, until well mixed. Fold in apple and butterscotch chips. Drop dough by walnut-size balls onto lightly greased baking sheets. Bake at 350 degrees for 12 minutes. Cool on a wire rack; spread with Frosting when cool. Makes 3 dozen.

Frosting:

2 c. powdered sugar
3 T. evaporated milk

3 T. butter, melted
1 t. cinnamon

Beat powdered sugar and evaporated milk with an electric mixer on medium speed until smooth. Gradually beat in butter and cinnamon until smooth.

A simple harvest decoration for cupcakes! Cut red, yellow and orange fruit-flavored snack rolls with leaf-shaped mini cookie cutters, then press the "leaves" onto frosted cupcakes.

Cookies, Cakes and Pies...*Oh My!*

Pumpkin Pie Ice Cream

Tracee Cummins
Georgetown, TX

Can't decide between pie and ice cream? Enjoy both! This fabulous dessert is a family favorite both in the summertime, when it's a cool treat on a hot day, and in autumn, when its spicy pumpkin flavor sweetens chilly nights. It's a welcome addition to a Thanksgiving dessert buffet too.

36 gingersnap cookies, divided
2 c. canned pumpkin
1/2 gal. vanilla ice cream,
   slightly softened
1 c. sugar
1 t. salt

1-1/8 t. cinnamon
1/2 t. ground ginger
1/8 t. nutmeg
1/2 c. chopped pecans
Garnish: whipped cream

Arrange half of the gingersnaps in the bottom of a 13"x9" baking pan; set aside. In a bowl, combine all ingredients except pecans and garnish; mix until well blended. Fold in pecans. Carefully spread over gingersnaps in pan; top with remaining gingersnaps. Cover and freeze overnight. Let stand at room temperature for several minutes, until slightly thawed; cut into squares. Serve topped with whipped cream. Makes 18 servings.

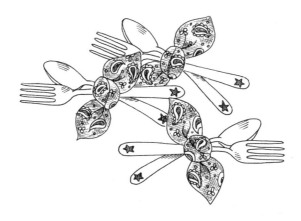

Give tonight's table a little flair...knot a cheery bandanna around each set of flatware. Bandannas come in so many bright colors, everyone can choose their own favorite.

Fudge Brownie Muffins

Vickie
Gooseberry Patch

We love these chocolatey muffins! They're made from simple ingredients I usually have in the pantry. Tuck them into lunchboxes, or serve them up as an after-school snack or even a breakfast treat.

1/2 c. butter, sliced
1/4 c. baking cocoa
2 eggs, lightly beaten
1 c. sugar
1 t. vanilla extract

3/4 c. all-purpose flour
1 t. cinnamon
1/4 c. chopped pecans
Garnish: semi-sweet
   chocolate chips

Combine butter and cocoa in a 2-cup glass measuring cup; microwave at high for one minute, or until butter melts. Set aside. In a large bowl, combine eggs, sugar and vanilla; beat well. Add butter mixture, flour and cinnamon; stir just until blended. Fold in pecans. Line 10 muffin cups with paper liners; spray lightly with non-stick vegetable spray. Spoon batter into cups, filling 2/3 full. Top each muffin with 6 to 8 chocolate morsels. Bake at 350 degrees for 20 minutes. Immediately remove muffins to a wire rack; cool. Makes 10 muffins.

For a clever party idea, line vintage trick-or-treat pails with wax paper and fill with easy-to-nibble cookies or candies.

Cookies, Cakes and Pies...*Oh My!*

Autumn Apple Brownies

Judy Lange
Imperial, PA

These brownies are such a treat in the fall. My family requests them as soon as the weather gets cool.

1 c. butter
2 c. sugar
2 eggs, beaten
2 c. all-purpose flour
1 t. baking powder

1 t. baking soda
2 t. cinnamon
3 c. apples, peeled, cored and thinly sliced

In a bowl, blend together butter and sugar; add eggs and mix well. In another bowl, combine flour, baking powder, baking soda and cinnamon; mix well. Add flour mixture to butter mixture; stir well. Fold in apples. Spread into a greased 13"x9" baking pan. Bake at 350 degrees for 40 to 50 minutes. Cut into squares. Makes one dozen.

Trail Mix Bars

Jill Ball
Highland, UT

One day I was looking for an alternative to crispy rice treats to take to my son's soccer game. I decided to add some nuts and dried fruit. They're a little heartier than the original...kids love them!

9-oz. pkg. marshmallows
2 T. olive oil
1 T. water
4 c. crispy rice cereal

2 c. favorite nut & fruit trail mix, with mini chocolate chips and mini pretzels if desired

In a large saucepan over medium heat, combine marshmallows, oil and water. Cook and stir until marshmallows are completely melted. Fold in cereal and trail mix. Press mixture into a greased 13"x9" baking pan; cool. Cut into bars; store in an airtight container. Makes 1-1/2 dozen.

Send a care package of cookies to college students so they arrive just before final exams...sure to bring smiles!

Harvest
Homestyle Meals

Cinnamon Apple Cookies

Dawn Dhooghe
Concord, NC

Every year my husband, daughter and I go apple picking. We come home with bushels of apples and the baking begins! This is the first recipe I pull out of my tattered box, the recipe that says "fall" to us.

1/2 c. butter, softened
1-1/4 c. brown sugar, packed
1 egg, lightly beaten
2 c. all-purpose flour
1/2 t. baking powder
1/2 t. baking soda
1/4 t. salt

1-1/2 t. cinnamon
1/4 t. nutmeg
1/4 c. milk
1-1/4 c. apples, peeled, cored
  and diced
1 c. cinnamon baking chips

In a large bowl, with an electric mixer on medium speed, beat butter and brown sugar until light and fluffy. Add egg; beat until blended well and set aside. In another bowl, combine flour, baking powder, baking soda, salt and spices. Add half of flour mixture to butter mixture; stir until mixed well. Add milk; mix well. Fold in apples and baking chips. Drop dough by tablespoonfuls onto lightly greased baking sheets, 2 inches apart. Bake at 375 degrees for 12 to 17 minutes, until cookies start to crust over and a toothpick tests done. Let cookies stand on baking sheets for 5 minutes; remove to a wire rack. Spread Glaze over warm cookies. Makes 2 dozen.

Glaze:

1-1/2 c. powdered sugar
1/2 t. vanilla extract

1 to 2 T. milk

Combine powdered sugar, vanilla and enough milk to form a smooth glaze.

Tie a stack of 3 big cookies together with a length of jute and set in the center of a dinner plate for a sweet surprise.

Cookies, Cakes and Pies...*Oh My!*

Warm Banana Bread Cobbler

Lisa Green
Parkersburg, WV

We love to sit around an autumn campfire, telling stories and enjoying this comforting cobbler.

1-1/2 c. self-rising flour, divided
1 c. sugar
3/4 c. milk
1/2 c. butter, melted
1 t. vanilla extract
4 ripe bananas, sliced

1 c. rolled oats, uncooked
3/4 c. brown sugar, packed
1/2 c. butter, softened
1/2 c. chopped walnuts
Garnish: vanilla ice cream

In a bowl, stir together one cup flour and sugar. Add milk, melted butter and vanilla; stir until smooth. Spread batter evenly in a buttered rectangular 3-quart casserole dish. Top with sliced bananas; set aside. In a separate large bowl, combine oats, brown sugar and remaining flour. With a pastry cutter, cut in softened butter until crumbly; stir in walnuts. Sprinkle mixture over bananas. Bake at 375 degrees for 25 to 30 minutes, until set and golden. Serve warm, topped with ice cream. Serves 12.

Little ones love to help out in the kitchen, so tuck a set of measuring spoons, oven mitt and mini rolling pin in the pocket of a child-size apron...everything a little helper needs.

Cranberry Jewel Bars

Cynthia Bullington
Rancho Cucamonga, CA

You don't need to wait for the holidays to eat these scrumptious bars. My family loves them year 'round!

2 c. all-purpose flour
1-1/2 c. rolled oats, uncooked
3/4 c. plus 1 T. light brown
   sugar, packed and divided
1 c. chilled butter
14-oz. can sweetened
   condensed milk

1 c. ricotta cheese
2 eggs, beaten
1-1/2 t. vanilla extract
1 t. orange zest
1 T. cornstarch
14-oz. can whole-berry
   cranberry sauce

In a large bowl, combine flour, oats and 3/4 cup sugar; mix well. Cut in butter until crumbly. Set aside 2 cups of crumb mixture. Press remaining crumbs firmly into the bottom of a lightly greased 13"x9" baking pan; bake at 350 degrees for 15 minutes. Meanwhile, in a separate bowl, beat condensed milk, cheese, eggs, vanilla and orange zest with an electric mixer on medium speed until smooth. Spread mixture evenly over prepared crust. In a small bowl, combine remaining brown sugar and cornstarch; stir in cranberry sauce. Spoon over cheese layer. Top with reserved crumb mixture. Bake at 350 degrees for 40 minutes, or until lightly golden. Cool; refrigerate. Cut into bars. Keep refrigerated. Makes 3 dozen.

Cooler weather and longer evenings are a cozy time just right for curling up with a good book. Keep several of your favorites on a table next to a cozy chair, brew a cup of hot tea and sit back to enjoy.

Cookies, Cakes and Pies...*Oh My!*

Black Walnut Dream Bars

Cynthia Copeland
Atlantic, IA

This is my mom's recipe, which she'd make to take to gatherings. There are never any left! These have been a favorite for a long time.

1 c. plus 2 T. all-purpose flour
1-1/2 c. brown sugar, packed
  and divided
1/2 c. butter, softened
1-1/4 c. sweetened flaked
  coconut

1 c. black walnuts, chopped
2 eggs, beaten
1/2 t. baking powder
1/4 t. salt
1 t. vanilla extract
Garnish: powdered sugar

In a bowl, combine one cup flour, 1/2 cup brown sugar and butter; mix well. Spread in an ungreased 13"x9" baking pan. Bake at 350 degrees for 15 minutes, or until lightly golden. In a separate bowl, combine remaining flour, remaining brown sugar and all other ingredients except garnish; spread over baked layer and bake for 20 minutes longer. Cut into bars; roll in powdered sugar. Makes 2 dozen.

A charming gift for anyone! Arrange Black Walnut Dream Bars on a mini cutting board. Wrap with clear plastic wrap to keep extra fresh, and tie a big checkered ribbon around the handle.

Harvest
Homestyle Meals

Monster Cookies

Julie Evink
Morris, MN

Derek, my best friend from high school, introduced me to this recipe, and it's been a staple in my kitchen ever since!

1/2 c. butter
1-1/2 c. creamy peanut butter
1 c. brown sugar, packed
1 c. sugar
3 eggs, beaten
1 t. corn syrup
1 t. vanilla extract

2 t. baking soda
4-1/2 c. quick-cooking oats, uncooked
1 c. peanut butter chips or semi-sweet chocolate chips
1 c. candy-coated chocolates

Combine all ingredients except chips and chocolates in a large bowl; mix well. Fold in chips and chocolates; let stand for 30 minutes. Drop dough by rounded teaspoonfuls onto greased baking sheets. Bake at 325 degrees for 12 minutes; remove from oven before cookies look done. Let stand on baking sheets for 5 minutes; remove to a wire rack and let cool. Makes 3 dozen.

Glorified Grahams

Robbi Buckles
South Lyon, MI

When I was a little girl, my mom made these often because they were so fast and simple to prepare. We all just loved them. Now that I have my own family and grandchildren, I carry on the tradition. These are always a favorite at potlucks and bake sales too.

24 graham cracker squares
1/2 c. butter, melted

1/2 c. brown sugar, packed
1 c. chopped pecans

Spray a 15"x10" jelly-roll pan with non-stick vegetable spray. Line pan with crackers; set aside. Combine melted butter and brown sugar in a bowl; mix well and spoon over graham crackers. Sprinkle with pecans. Bake at 350 degrees for about 12 minutes. Remove to a wire rack and cool. Makes 2 dozen.

Cookies, Cakes and Pies...*Oh My!*

Salted Peanut Cookies

Lenore Bricco
Miles City, MT

This is a yummy recipe...the peanuts and corn flakes give these cookies a great taste!

1 c. brown sugar, packed	1 t. baking powder
1 c. sugar	1 t. baking soda
1 c. shortening	1 c. rolled oats, uncooked
2 eggs, beaten	1 c. corn flake cereal, crushed
1 t. vanilla extract	1 c. salted Spanish peanuts
2 c. all-purpose flour	Garnish: additional sugar

In a large bowl, blend together sugars and shortening; stir in eggs and vanilla. Add flour, baking powder, baking soda and oats; mix well. Add crushed cereal and peanuts; stir well. Cover and chill for 30 minutes. Roll dough into one-inch balls; dip into sugar. Place balls on ungreased baking sheets. Bake at 370 degrees for 8 minutes. Makes 2 dozen.

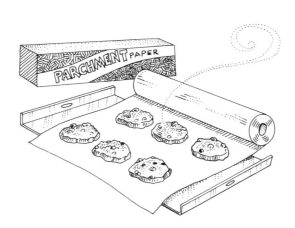

If you're baking lots of cookies and only have one baking sheet, simply line it with parchment paper. As each batch of cookies comes out of the oven, lift off the paper (cookies and all) onto a wire rack. Cool the hot baking sheet under running water and pat it dry... ready for you to add the next batch!

Harvest
Homestyle Meals

Carolyn's Pear Pie

Carolyn Irvine
Bay City, TX

I can't wait to pick pears each fall, so I can make this yummy pie!

5 c. Bosc or Anjou pears, cored
   and sliced
Optional: 1/2 c. raisins
2 T. plus 1 t. all-purpose flour
1/3 c. brown sugar, packed

1-1/4 t. cinnamon
1/4 t. nutmeg
1/4 t. salt
1 T. lemon juice
9-inch pie crust, unbaked

In a bowl, combine all ingredients except crust; mix well. Pour pear mixture into unbaked pie crust. Sprinkle Crumb Topping over pie. Bake at 400 degrees for 30 to 35 minutes, until lightly golden and pears are tender. Makes 8 servings.

Crumb Topping:

1/2 c. rolled oats, uncooked
1/2 c. brown sugar, packed
1/4 c. all-purpose flour
1/4 t. nutmeg

1/2 t. cinnamon
1/4 c. butter
1/2 c. chopped walnuts

Combine oats, sugar, flour and spices. Cut in butter until crumbly; fold in walnuts.

Invite family & friends to a dessert social. Everyone brings a pie,
a cake or another favorite dessert...you provide the ice cream
for topping and a pot of hot coffee. Sure to be delicious fun!

Cookies, Cakes and Pies...*Oh My!*

Texas Turtle Toasted Pecan Pie

Lisa Johnson
Hallsville, TX

My mama has made this rich Turtle Pie for years. Tastes as good the millionth time as it did the first time! To save time, use a purchased, chocolate pie crust, in place of the chocolate cookies and butter.

1-1/2 c. chocolate cookie crumbs
1/3 c. butter, melted
1-1/4 c. semi-sweet chocolate
   chips
1 c. evaporated milk
1/8 t. salt
1 c. mini marshmallows
1 qt. vanilla ice cream, divided
18 to 20 pecan halves, toasted
Garnish: caramel sauce

Stir together cookie crumbs and butter in a bowl. Press mixture into a 9" deep-dish pie plate. Cover and freeze for 15 minutes, until set. Meanwhile, combine chocolate chips, evaporated milk, salt and marshmallows in a heavy saucepan. Cook over low heat, stirring constantly, until melted, thickened and smooth. Remove from heat; set aside to cool. Spread 2 cups of ice cream into crust; cover and freeze for 30 minutes. Pour half of chocolate mixture over ice cream layer; cover and freeze again for about 30 minutes. Repeat step with remaining ice cream and chocolate mixture. Cover and freeze. At serving time, press pecan halves into the top of pie. Serve with caramel sauce. Makes 8 servings.

Toting a pie to a cookout or party? A bamboo steamer basket is just the thing...depending on its basket size, you may even be able to carry 2 pies at once.

Frosted Cut-Out Cookies

Traci Reed
Alexandria, PA

Being a stay-at-home mom for many years, my kids and I have experimented with many cut-out cookie recipes. This is one of our favorites. The frosting adds an extra sweet touch.

1 c. butter, softened	1 t. baking powder
1 c. sugar	2 T. orange juice
1 egg, beaten	1 T. vanilla extract
2-1/2 c. all-purpose flour	Optional: candy sprinkles

Combine butter, sugar and egg in a large bowl; beat with an electric mixer on medium speed until creamy. Add flour, baking powder, orange juice and vanilla; beat until well mixed. Cover and refrigerate dough until firm, 2 hours to overnight. Roll out dough on a lightly floured surface, 1/4-inch thick. Cut out with cookie cutters as desired. Bake at 400 degrees for 6 to 10 minutes, until lightly golden. Remove cookies to a wire rack. Frost and decorate cooled cookies, if desired. Makes about 2-1/2 dozen.

Frosting:

3 c. powdered sugar	1 to 2 T. milk
1/3 c. butter, softened	Optional: several drops food
1 t. vanilla extract	coloring

Combine powdered sugar, butter and vanilla in a large bowl. Beat with an electric mixer on low speed until smooth. Gradually beat in milk to desired spreading consistency. Tint with food coloring, if desired.

Mix up some orange frosting for Halloween cookies...it's like magic!
Simply add 6 drops yellow and 2 drops red food coloring to
a small bowl of white frosting.

Cookies, Cakes and Pies...*Oh My!*

Jam Bar Squares

Romelda Nickerson
Nova Scotia, Canada

These buttery squares of shortbread are easy and sure to become a favorite. Use any flavor of jam you like.

1 c. butter, room temperature
1 c. brown sugar, packed
1 egg, beaten
1 t. almond extract
2 c. all-purpose flour

1/2 t. salt
1/4 c. favorite fruit jam, any
  large chunks removed
1/3 to 1/2 c. sweetened flaked
  coconut

In a large bowl, beat butter and brown sugar with an electric mixer on medium speed until creamy. Beat in egg and extract until blended. Beat in flour and salt until well mixed. Press dough into a lightly greased 9"x9" baking pan. Bake at 350 degrees for 30 to 35 minutes, until golden. Remove from oven. Spread with jam; sprinkle with coconut. Cool completely and cut into small squares. Makes 2 to 3 dozen.

Jams and preserves keep well, so pick up a few jars of local specialties like strawberry, peach or boysenberry when on vacation or visiting farmstands. You'll be well stocked to bake up jam bars and thumbprint cookies!

Oatmeal Apple Cake

Ruby Jackson
Magazine, AR

This cake is moist and delightful. The recipe has been enjoyed in my family for many years. It won the prize for "Best of Taste" in our church's baking contest. It makes two pans...perfect for sharing!

1-1/4 c. boiling water
1 c. rolled oats, uncooked
1/3 c. butter
1 c. sugar
1 c. brown sugar, packed

1 c. applesauce
2 eggs, beaten
1-1/2 c. all-purpose flour
1 t. baking soda
1 t. cinnamon

In a large bowl, pour boiling water over oats and butter. Let stand for 20 minutes. Add remaining ingredients in the order given, stirring after each. Divide batter between 2 greased 8"x8" baking pans. Bake at 350 degrees for 30 minutes, or until a toothpick inserted into cake comes out clean. Cool; spread with hot Coconut-Pecan Frosting. Makes 2 pans, 8 servings per pan.

Coconut-Pecan Frosting:

6 T. butter
1/4 c. milk
1/2 c. sugar
1 egg, beaten

1 t. vanilla extract
1/2 t. salt
1 c. sweetened flaked coconut
1 c. chopped pecans

In a saucepan, combine butter, milk and sugar. Bring to a boil over medium heat; cook until mixture starts to thicken, stirring often. Place egg in a bowl; add one to 2 tablespoons of hot mixture to egg, beating constantly. Add egg mixture to mixture in pan. Cook 2 minutes more, stirring constantly. Stir in remaining ingredients.

Toasted coconut makes a great garnish for cakes! Place coconut in a dry skillet and heat over medium-low heat. Cook and stir until lightly toasted, about 3 minutes.

Holiday Pineapple Cake

Connie Lewis
Liberal, KS

This is a special recipe from a sister-in-law of mine. She has since passed on, but every time I make this cake, I think of her. It is truly scrumptious and you'll want to make it often.

20-oz. can crushed pineapple
2 c. all-purpose flour
1-1/2 c. sugar
1 t. baking soda
2 eggs, beaten
1/2 c. brown sugar, packed

1/2 c. chopped walnuts
1 c. margarine
1 c. evaporated milk
1 c. sugar
1 t. vanilla extract

In a large bowl, blend together pineapple with juice, flour, sugar, baking soda and eggs. Pour batter into a greased 13"x9" baking pan. In a separate bowl, mix together brown sugar and walnuts; sprinkle over batter. Bake at 350 degrees for 30 minutes, or until cake tests done with a toothpick; remove from oven. In a saucepan over medium heat, combine remaining ingredients. Bring to a boil; boil for 3 minutes. Pour hot mixture over cake. Serves 12 to 15.

To quickly break up walnuts and pecans, place whole nuts into a plastic zipping bag and pound with a meat mallet or rolling pin until desired size.

Harvest
Homestyle Meals

Butterscotch Apple Crisp

Laura Fredlund
Papillion, NE

*Butterscotch and baked apples...it can't get any better
than that! This dessert is a hit with everyone I share
it with...I am asked for the recipe every time.*

8 c. apples, peeled, cored
   and sliced
1 c. brown sugar, packed

2 T. all-purpose flour
1/2 c. milk
1 c. water

Combine all ingredients in a large bowl; mix well. Spread in an
ungreased 13"x9" baking pan. Crumble Topping over apple mixture.
Bake at 350 degrees until golden and bubbly, 45 to 50 minutes. Makes
8 to 10 servings.

Topping:

2 3.4-oz. pkgs. cook & serve
   butterscotch pudding mix
1-1/3 c. all-purpose flour
1 c. rolled oats, uncooked

1/2 c. sugar
1 c. butter, melted
2 t. cinnamon
1 t. salt

Combine dry pudding mixes and remaining ingredients;
mix until crumbly.

You wouldn't believe,
On All Hallow Eve
What lots of fun we can make,
With apples to bob,
And nuts on the hob,
And a ring-and-thimble cake.
– Carolyn Wells

Cookies, Cakes and Pies...*Oh My!*

Easy Breezy Pineapple-Cherry Cobbler

Shannon Fisher
Marion Heights, PA

This is an easy and delicious dessert that you can adjust for any special needs your family may have. I use no-sugar-added cherry filling, pineapple in natural juice and sugar-free cake mix for my husband who is diabetic.

21-oz. can cherry pie filling
20-oz. can crushed pineapple
18-oz. pkg. yellow cake mix

Optional: chopped walnuts
1/2 c. butter, melted
Garnish: vanilla ice cream

In a greased 13"x9" baking pan, combine pie filling and undrained pineapple. Sprinkle with dry cake mix and walnuts, if using; drizzle with melted butter. Bake at 350 degrees for 30 to 35 minutes. Serve warm, topped with ice cream. Makes 8 to 10 servings.

Beth's Quick & Easy Fruit Cobbler

Cynthia Dodge
Queen Creek, AZ

One of my best friends gave me this super-quick recipe over 25 years ago. It had been in her family for years before that. We love it too!

1 c. all-purpose flour
1 c. sugar
1 c. milk
1/2 c. margarine, melted

21-oz. can favorite fruit
  pie filling
Garnish: vanilla ice cream or
  whipped topping

In a bowl, gently toss together flour, sugar, milk and margarine. Spoon batter into a greased 8"x8" glass baking pan. Add pie filling over batter by spoonfuls. Bake at 350 degrees for 45 to 50 minutes, until golden. Serve warm, garnished as desired. Serves 4 to 6.

Black Magic Cake

Billie Jean Elliott
Woodsfield, OH

If you like chocolate, this is a recipe you will love. This recipe was given me by my sister-in-law Harriet. The cake is moist and yummy, easy to make and can be mixed up in 15 minutes or less. Thanks for sharing, Harriet!

1-3/4 c. all-purpose flour
2 c. sugar
3/4 c. baking cocoa
1 t. baking powder
2 t. baking soda
1 t. salt

2 eggs, beaten
1 c. strong black coffee
1 c. buttermilk
1/2 c. oil
1 t. vanilla extract

In a large bowl, mix together flour, sugar, cocoa, baking powder, baking soda and salt. Add remaining ingredients. Beat with an electric mixer on medium speed for 2 minutes; batter will be thin. Pour batter into a greased and floured 13"x9" baking pan or two 9" round cake pans. Bake at 350 degrees for 35 to 40 minutes, until cake tests done with a toothpick. Cool completely; spread Frosting over cake, or assemble layers with Frosting. Makes 12 servings.

Frosting:

1/2 c. margarine
2 1-oz. sqs. unsweetened baking
  chocolate, melted

3 c. powdered sugar
2 t. vanilla extract
3 T. milk

Beat together all ingredients.

For blue ribbon-perfect chocolate cakes with no white streaks, dust greased pans with baking cocoa instead of flour.

Cookies, Cakes and Pies...*Oh My!*

Mom's Pumpkin Pie

Cindy Pogge
Kanawha, IA

This is the pumpkin pie my mother always made, and it is the only one we ever use. When the family was all together, we would make as many as 15 of these pies every Thanksgiving! And of course, we use only real whipped cream on top.

15-oz. can pumpkin
1-1/8 t. cinnamon
3/4 c. brown sugar, packed
1/2 c. sugar
3 eggs, beaten

1 c. evaporated milk
1 t. vanilla extract
1/8 t. salt
9-inch pie crust, unbaked
Garnish: whipped cream

Combine pumpkin and cinnamon in a large bowl; mix well. Add sugars and mix well. Add eggs, milk, vanilla and salt; blend thoroughly. Spoon mixture into pie crust. Bake at 425 degrees for 15 minutes; reduce heat to 350 degrees. Continue baking for 40 to 50 minutes, until a knife tip inserted in the center comes out clean. Cool; garnish with whipped cream. Serves 6 to 8.

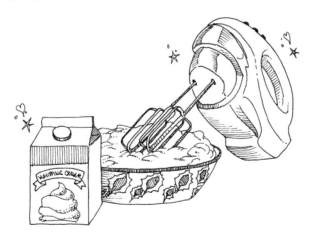

Top your best homemade desserts with real whipped cream...
it's simple. With an electric mixer on high speed, beat one cup
whipping cream until soft peaks form. Add one tablespoon
powdered sugar and one teaspoon vanilla extract. Continue
to beat until stiff peaks form...enjoy!

Harvest
Homestyle Meals

Chocolate-Covered Cherry Bars

James Bohner
Harrisburg, PA

If you like chocolate-covered cherries, you will love this simple yet elegant recipe. Try adding white chocolate chips or mix half chocolate and half white chocolate chips...yummy!

18-1/2 oz. pkg. chocolate
    cake mix
2 eggs, beaten
1/2 c. oil
2 T. water

12-oz. pkg. semi-sweet chocolate
    chips
1/2 c. maraschino cherries,
    drained and chopped

Mix all ingredients together in a large bowl. Pour batter into a greased 13"x9" baking pan. Bake at 350 degrees for 20 to 25 minutes. Cool for one hour; cut into bars. Makes 1-1/2 dozen.

Milk Chocolate Brownies

Becky Holsinger
Belpre, OH

I love these quick & easy brownies! The house smells so good while they are baking.

12-oz. pkg. semi-sweet
    chocolate chips
14-oz. can sweetened
    condensed milk

2 T. oil
Optional: 1 c. chopped nuts
2 c. biscuit baking mix

Melt chocolate chips in a saucepan over low heat; set aside. Combine condensed milk and oil in a large bowl; fold in nuts, if using. Stir in melted chocolate and baking mix. Spread batter in a greased 13"x9" baking pan. Bake at 375 degrees for 20 to 25 minutes. Cool slightly; cut into squares. Makes 1-1/2 dozen.

A little of what you fancy does you good.
– Marie Lloyd

Cookies, Cakes and Pies... *Oh My!*

Pecan Tarts

Judy Taylor
Butler, MO

I shared this recipe when I was "Cook of the Week" in our local newspaper many, many years ago. My daughter was about three years old at the time, and the photo in the paper shows the two of us along with our Pecan Tarts. Whenever I make these, I always think of that picture.

1 c. butter, softened	2 c. all-purpose flour
2/3 c. cream cheese, softened	1/2 t. salt

In a large bowl, blend together butter and cream cheese. Add flour and salt; mix well. Roll dough into walnut-size balls. Press into 1-3/4 inch tart pans to form crusts; be careful not to make crusts too thick. Spoon Pecan Filling into tart crusts, filling each about 2/3 full. Bake at 350 degrees for 20 to 25 minutes. Makes 3 dozen.

Pecan Filling:

3 eggs, beaten	1/3 c. butter, melted
2/3 c. sugar	1 c. light or dark corn syrup
1/2 t. salt	1 c. pecans, coarsely chopped

In a large bowl, combine eggs, sugar, salt, butter and syrup. Beat with an electric mixer on low speed until smooth. Stir in pecans.

Don't hide a pretty glass cake stand in the cupboard! Use it to show off several of Mom's best dessert plates or arrange colorful, seasonal fruit on top.

Stephanie's Fried Apple Pies

Stephanie Jackson
Falkner, MS

When I was little, Momma would make these little pies,
and we could hardly wait for them to cool. So good!

2 baking apples, peeled,
  cored and diced
1/3 c. sugar
1/2 t. cinnamon
2 c. all-purpose flour

1 t. salt
1/2 c. shortening
1/2 c. cold water
1 c. oil
Garnish: powdered sugar

In a saucepan, combine apples, sugar and cinnamon. Cook over low heat until soft, stirring occasionally. Mash with a fork to form a thick applesauce; remove from heat. In a large bowl, sift together flour and salt; cut in shortening. Add water; mix with fork. Roll out dough on a floured surface, about 1/8-inch thick. Cut out dough into circles with a 4-inch round cookie cutter. Spoon a heaping tablespoon of apple mixture into each dough circle. Moisten edges with cold water; fold in half and press edges with a fork. Heat oil in a large skillet over medium-high heat. Fry pies, a few at a time, 2 to 3 minutes per side, until golden. Drain on paper towels; sprinkle with powdered sugar. Makes 6 servings.

Which apple to pick? The tastiest pie apples are Rome, Jonathan, Fuji and Granny Smith. For salads, try McIntosh, Red Delicious, Empire and Gala. Combine a variety of sweet and tart apples for the richest flavor.

Cookies, Cakes and Pies...*Oh My!*

Spicy Pumpkin-Chocolate Chip Bundt Cake

Susan Willie
Ridgecrest, NC

The first time I made this cake, it was a big hit!
Easy to make and very good.

18-1/2 oz. pkg. spice cake mix
2 eggs, beaten
1/2 c. water
1/2 c. oil
1/2 c. cream cheese, softened
1 c. canned pumpkin

1 t. cinnamon
1/2 t. ground ginger
6-oz. pkg. semi-sweet chocolate
  chips
16-oz. can cream cheese frosting

In a large bowl, combine dry cake mix, eggs, water and oil; blend well. Add cream cheese, pumpkin and spices. Beat with an electric mixer on medium speed for about 2 minutes, until well blended. Stir in chocolate chips. Pour batter into a greased Bundt® pan. Bake at 350 degrees for 45 minutes, or until a toothpick inserted in center comes out clean. Cool cake in pan for 10 minutes. Turn out cake onto a wire rack; cool completely. Spread frosting on top and halfway down the sides of cake. Makes 12 servings.

Add some retro charm the next time you bake a Bundt® cake.
When serving, fill a vintage milk bottle with water and use it to
hold seasonal flowers in the center of the cake.

Harvest Homestyle Meals

Kary's Pumpkin Cobbler

Kary Ross
Searcy, AR

I adapted this recipe using my mother's pumpkin pie recipe. So easy and quick...the flavors remind everyone of the Thanksgiving season!

29-oz. can pumpkin
2 t. cinnamon
1 t. pumpkin pie spice
2 t. nutmeg
3 eggs, beaten
1 c. brown sugar, packed

12-oz. can evaporated milk
1/2 t. salt
18-1/2 oz. pkg. yellow cake mix
  with pudding
1/2 c. butter, melted
1/2 c. chopped pecans

Mix together pumpkin and spices in a bowl; set aside. In a large bowl, beat together eggs, brown sugar, evaporated milk and salt. Add pumpkin mixture to egg mixture; blend well. Pour batter into a greased 13"x9" baking pan. In a separate bowl, mix dry cake mix with melted butter; drop by spoonfuls over pumpkin mixture. Pan will be very full. Bake at 350 degrees for 50 minutes. Sprinkle with pecans; bake for another 10 minutes. Makes 8 to 10 servings.

Spend the day catching up on scrapbooking! Girlfriends, grandmas, aunts and moms will enjoy creating a favorite recipe book. It's easy to include everyone's favorites by making color copies of recipe cards in their handwriting.

Cookies, Cakes and Pies... *Oh My!*

Pecan Praline-Apple Pie

Sheila Wilson
Waco, TX

*I came up with this recipe one day several years ago. I wanted to
make an apple pie with a different spin on it. It turned out
really good...hope you like this recipe too!*

2 9-inch pie crusts
6 c. tart apples, peeled, cored
   and sliced
1 c. sugar
2 to 3 T. all-purpose flour

1 t. cinnamon
1/8 t. salt
2 T. lemon juice
2 T. butter, diced

Arrange one pie crust in a 9" pie plate; set aside. In a large bowl, mix
together apples, sugar, flour, cinnamon, salt and lemon juice until
apples are well coated. Spoon apple mixture into pie crust; dot with
butter. Place remaining crust over apple mixture. Press together to seal
and flute edges; make several slits with a knife tip. Bake at 425 degrees
for 20 to 25 minutes, until apples are tender. Spoon Praline Topping
over crust. Return to oven; bake for another 20 minutes, or until
topping is golden. Serves 6 to 8.

Praline Topping:

2 T. butter
1-1/2 c. dark brown sugar,
   packed

1 c. chopped pecans

In a saucepan over medium-low heat, melt butter with brown sugar; stir
well. When sugar starts to caramelize slightly, add pecans, stirring
constantly, until golden.

Jazz up homemade apple desserts in a jiffy. Top with a drizzle
of warm caramel sauce...scrumptious!

Caramel Apple-Cinnamon Bars

Christina Burrell
North Richland Hills, TX

I created this recipe shortly after I got married, to combine several of our favorite flavors...caramel apples and cinnamon-sugar oatmeal. Now it's our annual tradition to host a fall gathering for friends and neighbors, serving these bars with hot cocoa and hot apple cider. These bars also taste delicious served warm, topped with vanilla ice cream and drizzled with caramel topping.

1 c. brown sugar, packed
1/2 c. butter, softened
1/4 c. shortening
1-1/2 c. quick-cooking oats, uncooked
1-3/4 c. plus 3 T. all-purpose flour, divided

1/2 t. baking soda
1 t. salt
4-1/2 c. tart apples, peeled, cored and coarsely chopped
3 T. cinnamon-sugar, divided
14-oz. pkg. caramels, unwrapped

In a large bowl, combine brown sugar, butter and shortening. Stir in oats, 1-3/4 cups flour, baking soda and salt. Reserve 2 cups of oat mixture for topping. Press remaining oat mixture into an ungreased 13"x9" baking pan; set aside. In a separate bowl, toss together apples, remaining flour and one tablespoon cinnamon-sugar. Spread over oat mixture in pan and set aside. Cook caramels in a saucepan over low heat, stirring occasionally, until melted; pour evenly over apple mixture. Sprinkle with reserved oat mixture and remaining cinnamon-sugar, pressing lightly. Bake at 400 degrees for 25 to 30 minutes, until apples are tender and topping is golden. Cut into squares while still warm. Store, covered in refrigerator. Makes 3 dozen.

When whisking or beating ingredients in a bowl, a damp tea towel can hold the mixing bowl in place. Just twist the towel securely into a ring, around the base of the bowl.

Cookies, Cakes and Pies...*Oh My!*

Peanut Butter & Jam Bars

Becky Bruner
Virginia Beach, VA

I was a teenager when I began making these bars with my mom. They make such a pretty addition to any dessert tray! It's obvious by the tattered and stained recipe card that they have become a treasured favorite.

1/2 c. brown sugar, packed
1/2 c. sugar
1/2 c. shortening
1/2 c. creamy peanut butter
1 egg, beaten

1-1/4 all-purpose flour
1/2 t. baking powder
3/4 t. baking soda
1/2 c. red raspberry jam

In a large bowl, mix sugars, shortening, peanut butter and egg. Stir in flour, baking powder and baking soda. Reserve one cup of dough for topping. Press remaining dough into an ungreased 13"x9" baking pan; spread with jam. Crumble reserved dough and sprinkle over jam. Bake at 350 degrees for about 20 minutes, until golden. Cool; drizzle with Glaze. Cut into bars. Makes 3 dozen.

Glaze:

2 T. butter
1 c. powdered sugar

1 t. vanilla extract
1 to 2 T. hot water

Heat butter in a saucepan over low heat until melted; stir in powdered sugar and vanilla. Beat in hot water, one tablespoon at a time, until smooth and to desired consistency.

It's the perfect time of year to share some tasty treats with teachers, librarians and school bus drivers... let them know how much you appreciate them!

Harvest
Homestyle Meals

Devil's Food Drop Cookies

Cathy Callen
Lawton, OK

We loved to make these tasty cookies for our kids as a special treat. You can dress them up and take them to town with special touches to the frosting.

1/2 c. butter
1 c. brown sugar, packed
1 egg, beaten
1 t. vanilla extract
2 1-oz. sqs. unsweetened
   baking chocolate, melted

2 c. all-purpose flour
1/2 t. baking soda
1/4 t. salt
3/4 c. sour cream

In a large bowl, blend together butter and brown sugar. Beat in egg, vanilla and melted chocolate; set aside. In a separate bowl, sift together flour, baking soda and salt. Blend flour mixture into butter mixture alternately with sour cream. Drop dough by tablespoonfuls onto baking sheets lightly sprayed with non-stick vegetable spray. Bake at 350 degrees for 8 to 10 minutes. Remove cookies to a wire rack while still slightly warm. Spread each cookie with a small amount of Cocoa Frosting. Makes 2 dozen.

Cocoa Frosting:

1/4 c. butter, softened
2 T. baking cocoa
1/8 t. salt

1 c. powdered sugar
3 T. milk
1-1/2 t. vanilla extract

Blend together butter, cocoa and salt; set aside. In a separate bowl, combine powdered sugar, milk and vanilla. Add butter mixture to sugar mixture; blend until smooth.

A vintage black lunchbox makes a clever Halloween candy holder...just fill with tasty treats for little goblins to choose from.

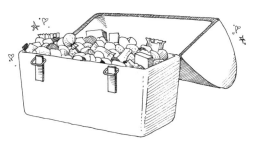

Cookies, Cakes and Pies...*Oh My!*

Rich Bread Pudding

Darla Bernabe-Sackman
Wentzville, MO

This is a delicious old-fashioned dessert. Top it with caramel sauce if you like, but I find it's usually sweet enough already! This freezes well...allow it to cool, then wrap with plastic wrap and then store in the freezer. Once removed from the freezer, allow to thaw and rewarm it in the oven or microwave.

4 c. whipping cream
5 egg yolks
1 c. sugar
1 t. vanilla extract
1 t. cinnamon
8-oz. pkg. cream cheese, room
    temperature

1/2 c. powdered sugar
1 to 2 T. milk
1 loaf French bread, cubed
Optional: 1/2 c. raisins

Warm cream in a heavy saucepan over low heat until small bubbles form; do not boil. Meanwhile, in a separate bowl, combine egg yolks and sugar; whisk until light yellow. Slowly whisk warm cream into yolk mixture; stir in vanilla and cinnamon. Cover and refrigerate about 30 minutes until cool, stirring occasionally. In a separate bowl, beat cream cheese with an electric mixer on medium speed until smooth. Turn mixer to low speed; beat in powdered sugar, adding enough milk to make a smooth consistency. Add to cream mixture; stir well and set aside. In a very large bowl, combine bread, cream mixture and raisins, if using. Allow bread to soak up cream mixture. Divide mixture evenly between 2 greased 9"x9" baking pans. Bake at 350 degrees for 25 to 30 minutes, until set and center is slightly wiggly. Pudding will continue to cook as it cools. Makes 2 pans; each serves 6 to 8.

Rich Bread Pudding is a delicious way to use up day-old bread. Try country-style bread, raisin bread or even leftover doughnuts and cinnamon buns for an extra-tasty dessert.

Sweet Potato Casserole

Tina Vawter
Sheridan, IN

This sweet potato casserole is like a dessert. My Grandma Ena made it every year for Thanksgiving dinner. We'd travel from Indiana to Kentucky to spend Thanksgiving with my grandparents, only missing a handful once our girls were born. When Grandma was no longer able to make the casserole, I continued to bring along the ingredients at Thanksgiving and made it for our dinner, with her nearby to "supervise" the mixture. My sweet grandma has since passed away, so now I make it each holiday in her memory. Somehow it comforts me while sitting around the table with the rest of the family. It's as if she is still right there with us.

3 c. sweet potatoes, peeled,
   cooked and mashed
1 c. sugar
1/2 t. salt
2 eggs, beaten

2-1/2 T. butter, melted
1/4 c. milk
1 t. vanilla extract
Optional: vanilla ice cream or
   whipped cream

In a large bowl, combine all ingredients except optional garnish. Mix well; transfer to a buttered 13"x9" glass baking pan. Crumble Pecan Topping over top. Bake at 350 degrees for 35 minutes, or until hot and golden. Garnish as desired. Makes 12 servings.

Pecan Topping:

1 c. brown sugar, packed
1/2 c. pecans, crushed

1/3 c. all-purpose flour
1/3 c. butter, melted

Mix together all ingredients until crumbly.

Write a sweet word of thanks or harvest quotes on strips of paper and fasten to the outside of glasses with double-sided tape. When Thanksgiving guests are seated, invite them to read the quote aloud.

Cookies, Cakes and Pies...*Oh My!*

Butter & Nut Pound Cake

Robyn Stroh
Calera, AL

When I was a little girl, my mom used to make this cake often. Once I became a teenager, I made it so often that I had the recipe memorized. Now that I am a wife and mother, this is my husband's favorite pound cake. It is so delicious!

1 c. butter, softened	2-1/2 c. all-purpose flour
2 c. sugar	1 c. milk
4 eggs	1 to 2 T. vanilla, butter &
1/2 c. self-rising flour	nut flavoring

In a large bowl, blend together butter and sugar until light and fluffy. Add eggs, one at a time, beating after each addition. Add self-rising flour; mix well. Add all-purpose flour alternately with milk, ending with flour. Beat until well combined after each addition. Stir in flavoring. Transfer batter to a greased and floured Bundt® pan. Bake at 325 degrees for one hour and 10 to 15 minutes. Makes 12 to 16 servings.

Coffee Punch

Liz Plotnick-Snay
Gooseberry Patch

Even better than iced coffee...perfect for dessert!

2 c. boiling water	1 gal. 2% milk
1 c. sugar	1/2 gal. vanilla ice cream
2-oz. jar instant coffee granules	1/2 gal. chocolate ice cream

In a bowl, stir together boiling water, sugar and instant coffee until dissolved. Cover and cool in refrigerator, 30 minutes to overnight. At serving time, pour coffee mixture into a punch bowl; add milk and ice cream. Stir until ice cream begins to melt. Serves 20.

Harvest Homestyle Meals

Apple Cider Cupcakes

Barb Bargdill
Gooseberry Patch

These delicious cupcakes are easy to whip up with ingredients you may already have in the pantry...no mix needed!

3 c. apple cider	1 t. baking soda
3/4 c. shortening	1/8 t. salt
1-3/4 c. sugar	1 t. cinnamon
2 eggs	1/8 t. ground cloves
2 c. all-purpose flour	16-oz. container vanilla frosting

Add cider to a large saucepan over medium-high heat; bring to a boil. Boil until cider cooks down to about 1-1/2 cups. Allow to cool. In a large bowl, with an electric mixer on medium speed, beat together shortening and sugar until fluffy. Beat in eggs, one at a time; set aside. Sift together flour, baking soda, salt and spices into shortening mixture. Stir in the reduced cider. Divide batter among 18 paper-lined muffin cups. Bake at 375 degrees for 25 minutes, or until a toothpick comes out clean. Cool cupcakes in tin on a wire rack. Spread cupcakes with frosting. Makes 1-1/2 dozen.

Campfire Apple Treat

Lynn Williams
Muncie, IN

Make as many as you like! Serve over ice cream or enjoy on its own.

1 apple, cored and thinly sliced	1 T. honey
1 T. golden raisins	cinnamon to taste
1 T. butter, softened	

Place apple slices on a long piece of heavy-duty aluminum foil; sprinkle with raisins and set aside. Blend butter and honey in a cup; spoon over fruit. Sprinkle with cinnamon. Wrap up foil, forming a packet. Grill over medium heat until apple is tender, 10 to 15 minutes, turning over once. Stir before serving. Serves one.

S'mores on the go...pack graham crackers, chocolate candy bars and a jar of marshmallow creme. Yum!

Cookies, Cakes and Pies...*Oh My!*

Candy Cookie Bark

Annette Ingram
Grand Rapids, MI

My kids collect so much candy during trick-or-treating that they can't eat it all. Then I bake up this recipe with the leftovers... turns it into a completely new treat for us!

16-1/2 oz. tube refrigerated chocolate chip cookie dough, sliced 1/4-inch thick
2-1/2 c. semi-sweet chocolate chips, divided
1-1/2 c. mini pretzel twists, broken

3 2-oz. chocolate-covered caramel peanut candy bars, chopped
1 c. candy corn
1-1/2 t. shortening

With moistened fingers, press cookie dough slices into a greased 15"x10" jelly-roll pan, forming a thin dough layer. Bake at 350 degrees for 10 minutes, or until golden. Cool completely, about 30 minutes. Add 2 cups chocolate chips to a microwave-safe bowl. Microwave, uncovered, on high for one to 2 minutes, until melted, stirring every 30 seconds. Spread melted chocolate over baked crust. Sprinkle with pretzels, candy bars and candy corn, pressing lightly. In a small microwave-safe bowl, microwave remaining chocolate chips and shortening, uncovered, on high for one minute, stirring after 30 seconds; drizzle over top. Cover lightly and refrigerate for 30 minutes, or until set. Break into 2-inch pieces. Makes 12 to 15 servings.

Make the sweetest harvest of "acorns" in a jiffy! With a dab of frosting, attach a mini vanilla wafer to a milk chocolate drop. Add a "stem" made from a bit of pretzel. Fill a bowl for nibbling, or top each dinner plate with 3 or 4 acorns.

INDEX

INDEX

INDEX

Find Gooseberry Patch
wherever you are!

www.gooseberrypatch.com

Call us toll-free at 1·800·854·6673

homecoming parades   colorful leaves

casual get-togethers

drives in the country

moonlit hayrides

craft fairs

crackling bonfires   community suppers

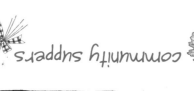

U.S. to Metric Recipe Equivalents

Volume Measurements

1/4 teaspoon	1 mL
1/2 teaspoon	2 mL
1 teaspoon	5 mL
1 tablespoon = 3 teaspoons	15 mL
2 tablespoons = 1 fluid ounce	30 mL
1/4 cup	60 mL
1/3 cup	75 mL
1/2 cup = 4 fluid ounces	125 mL
1 cup = 8 fluid ounces	250 mL
2 cups = 1 pint =16 fluid ounces	500 mL
4 cups = 1 quart	1 L

Weights

1 ounce	30 g
4 ounces	120 g
8 ounces	225 g
16 ounces = 1 pound	450 g

Oven Temperatures

300° F	150° C
325° F	160° C
350° F	180° C
375° F	190° C
400° F	200° C
450° F	230° C

Baking Pan Sizes

Square		*Loaf*	
8x8x2 inches	2 L = 20x20x5 cm	9x5x3 inches	2 L = 23x13x7 cm
9x9x2 inches	2.5 L = 23x23x5 cm	*Round*	
Rectangular		8x1-1/2 inches	1.2 L = 20x4 cm
13x9x2 inches	3.5 L = 33x23x5 cm	9x1-1/2 inches	1.5 L = 23x4 cm